THE RIGHT HAND OF GOD

THE RIGHT HAND OF GOD

Nelda Moffatt

The Right Hand of God examines the Bible and Christianity
in the context of history
from creation to the 21st century

TATE PUBLISHING
AND ENTERPRISES, LLC

Published by Tate Publishing & Enterprises, LLC
127 E. Trade Center Terrace | Mustang, Oklahoma 73064 USA
1.888.361.9473 | www.tatepublishing.com

Tate Publishing is committed to excellence in the publishing industry. The company reflects the philosophy established by the founders, based on Psalm 68:11,
"The Lord gave the word and great was the company of those who published it."

Book design copyright © 2015 by Tate Publishing, LLC. All rights reserved.
Cover design by Norlan Balazo
Interior design by Mary Jean Archival

Published in the United States of America

ISBN: 978-1-68142-315-9
1. Religion / Christian Theology / History
2. Religion / Christianity / History
15.04.22

Dedication

To my parents and grandparents, Marie and Hugo Bachle and
Therese and Friedrich Schlennstedt. They opened my mind to
the world and conveyed a strong sense of character and integrity
in me.

Acknowledgment

Part of my life was lived with gas lights, sad irons heated on a wood stove, and a phone that was an oak box on the wall. So I am very grateful for the twenty-first century electronic assistance that I received.

My son, Richard Moffatt, set up my manuscript in workable electronic form. My granddaughter, Laura Davis, inserted the maps and charts. She also encouraged me with content. She stated, "It is a concise perspective of the conjunction of history, science, and religion that many people, specifically millennials, are looking for today."

A one-page summary of *The Right Hand Of God*

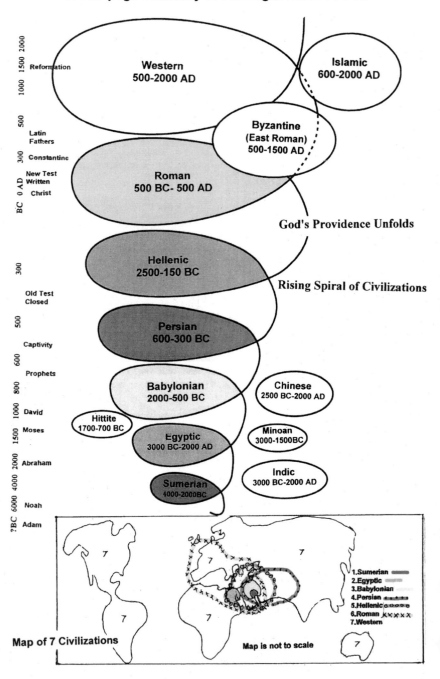

Contents

Preface

The *Right Hand of God* examines the Bible and Christianity in the context of history so the church may have an all-encompassing view of history and of the world within a metaphysical framework that includes all of knowledge yet is easy to understand.

The narrative is tersely written because no one has time for lengthy expositions. It is simplified, perhaps oversimplified, so that we may comprehend the overall framework without getting too consumed in details now. It also assumes a basic knowledge of the Bible.

The main purpose is to provide a deeper understanding of the Trinity.

Creator: through understanding evolution—physical, social, and spiritual—as God's pattern of creation.[1]

---

1. If slow step-by-step evolution *is* God's pattern of creation, are Christians who deny evolution flying in the face of God's basic principle of creative design?

Christ: through understanding the concept that the "Son of Man at the right hand of God" includes all of BC and AD history, plus Owen Barfield's idea that "all of history lies between the First and Third Persons of the Trinity."

Spirit: through understanding the importance of will or spirit as the third part of the heredity-environment-will equation so each person with an indwelling of the Holy Spirit may merge his will with God's will, his spirit with God's Spirit.

Finally, we will be able to enter the "age of integrity," when we have harmony between man and God (each individual of integrity with God), between man and man (throughout all of society), and between man and creation.

Such understanding, along with recognition of *one* God Almighty, who revealed Himself in the Trinity, may bring enough people to truly *know* God—to have unity and intimacy with Him—so the spiritual kingdom of God may indeed come to fulfillment in the twenty-first century.

1

God Almighty, El Shaddai, and His Creation

The Word Spoken Created

In the beginning was the Word, but the Word needed interpreting. Perhaps a fresh approach is needed in our interpretation so we may truly *know* God Almighty, whose Word *created*, whose Word *became flesh*, and whose Word *unsealed* may bring understanding to *all* of His people in all of His world.

While the Bible does not provide a definitive study of creation or of history, it is amazing the way a mere phrase can suggest and encompass an entire stage of development. We are only beginning to understand this, thanks to scientific and archeological discoveries of the twentieth century. Yet, ironically, the Bible may still be ahead of science.

Two remarkable phrases run through the first ten verses of Genesis: "separating" and "gathering" This separating and gathering together is the pattern of creation by which God began His long chain of physical evolution, which we are only beginning to understand.

In the last decade or so, we have started hearing about "dark energy" and "dark matter." A recent article stated that about 70 percent of the universe is dark energy, 25 percent is dark matter, and only 5 percent is matter as we know it. No one really knows what the two are, yet scientists seem to agree that dark energy is a force that pushes things—pushes the universe—apart. Isn't that the same as *separating*? Dark matter pulls things together. Isn't that the same as *gathering together*? These are the two underlying forces driving the universe. Separating and gathering together.

It seems like science is just now catching up with the Bible.

These two forces also started the long chain of physical evolution—the part we see. God first separated and gathered together on the *nuclear* level (i.e., the sub-subatomic level).

In the beginning, God created. He spoke, and His Word, His Spirit, moved over the face of the deep—over chaos. God said, "Let there be light." Since light is the only electromagnetic wave visible to the eye, what better way for the Bible to say that God created electromagnetic waves than His Words "let there be light"? How could the Bible writers have known what we would name electromagnetic waves when we discovered them—in the twentieth century?

In this first stage—or "day" that could be millions or billions of years—God separated and gathered together the light and dark of Day and Night. This would be the "light" of cumulative-gathering development that unfolded in the atoms and molecules of chemistry, which separated from the "dark" of its black hole opposite. (*Day* and *Night* with capital letters or in quotes in Genesis 1:5 is different from *day* and *night* with sun and moon in Genesis 1:14.)

In the second stage, or "day" of development, God separated and gathered together on the *astrophysical* level of the "sky." This is the cosmic level when gaseous nebulae separated into clumps that gathered together into galaxies of stars. In time, this included our Milky Way galaxy and our own solar system circling in an outer spiral of the Milky Way.

The third stage is the *geophysical* level of earth. About 4.5 billion years ago, rocks and asteroids circling the sun in our orbit gathered together to form our earth. In time, the core separated from the crust with a "fluid" mantle in between.

In the fourth stage of development, the earth was regulated. Its yearly orbit, its rotation for day and night, and its tilt for the seasons became dependable. This is when *day* and *night* with small letters is noted (Gen. 1:14). Scientists now believe an asteroid or "planetoid" the size of Mars collided with the earth with a glancing blow, or the earth would have blown up. This slowed the rotation of the earth for our twenty-four-hour day and night. The collision also caused an eruption of material that gathered together to form our moon. The moon has since kept the earth regulated and balanced on its axis with its tilt for the seasons. Again, science has caught up with the Bible.

The fifth stage was the *biophysical* level. This was possible after steam gathered into water, which fell into oceans that separated from dry land. About 3.5 billion years ago, the chain of life began. Cells evolved and gathered together into multicellular organisms that separated into plants and animals. Animals evolved in the order recorded, first in the sea and then on land.

Finally, in the late afternoon of the sixth day, God created man *in His own image* and gave him dominion and care of the earth and all the creatures.

Thus the Word "spoken" created order out of physical chaos.[1]

---

1.   Please see the next page for a chart of the geological eras. The eras read from the earliest at the bottom up to the most recent on top because that is the way the geological layers were laid down. Note that all the geo eras of the earth are named in relation to life—the zoic, even the Archeozoic, which was prelife.

Geological Chart[2]

Era	Years Ago	Geological Event	Most Significant Life Event
Psychozoic	10,000	7 Continents	*Age of Man* as historical man emerges. *Homo sapiens* established and poised for social-psyche development.
	40,000?		
	100,000		Real man evolves with large brain.
Ice Age at 800,000–10,000 years ago—cyclic with interglacial periods			
Cenozoic	1 million	6 continents	Preman exists as erect hunter-gatherer.
	70 million	5 continents	*Age of Mammals* as first placental species evolved, including earliest squirrel-sized primates.
Mesozoic	100 million	3 continents	Dinosaurs died while mammals of egg-laying and marsupial type spread. Also, flowering plants emerge.
	150 million	2 continents	*Age of Reptiles* as dinosaurs reign. Conifers replace earlier fern forests.
	200 million	1 continent	
Ice Age at 200 million years ago			

---

2. This chart is a simplified version because it does not show the epochs that each era is subdivided into. Also note the designation "Psychozoic" era for man's *conscious awareness*. Thanks for this name goes to Robert S. Dietz and John C. Holden in their article "The Break-Up of Pangea" (*Scientific American*, October 1970). Their article was included in the book *Continents Adrift*, which was compiled by *Scientific American* in 1972.

Paleozoic	300 million	1 continent	*Age of Amphibians* as reptiles and insects rise. Fern forests develop. Fish thrive.
	400 million		*Age of Fish* as land plants and animals leave water.
	500 million		First vertebrates, primitive fish
	600 million		Real life begins as marine invertebrates (oysters, shrimp) develop.
Ice Age at 600 million years ago			
Protozoic	1.5 billion		Multicellular organisms develop into protoplant and animal kingdoms.
	3.1 billion		Organic compounds form into ocean broth to become unicellular microorganisms of prelife.
Archeozoic	3.5 billion		Air and water released. Both "weather" earth's surface as oceans fill.
	4.5 billion		Earth formed. Heavier core separated from crystallizing crust with "plastic" mantle in between.

Generic Man

Paleontologists are still trying to discover where and when man took his last evolutionary step to become *Homo sapiens sapiens*. The second *sapiens* refers to man's psychic awareness. Did he take that last step is the East Mediterranean? One hundred thousand years ago?

He came out of Africa a fine specimen of physical evolution with two legs for erect carriage, with hands for tool dexterity, with eyes set for stereoscopic 3-D vision, and with a large brain equipped for survival.

19

Finally, man reached the point of awareness when his mind and spirit were awakened—when God breathed spirit into man! With the ability to think, he was able to *separate* and name animals, then objects and persons, and ultimately, ideas. These "names" were later gathered together and passed from generation to generation in a cumulative fund of knowledge. Cumulative is the key, for everything builds on what went before. That is evolution. And that is efficient. You do not have to start everything at zero and reinvent DNA or the alphabet or the wheel. Once is enough, *if* you build on it and pass it on to the next generation.

The Bible recognized the importance of the naming process. Generic man, not yet brand-name Adam, spent "days" at naming. During the thousands of years of speech development, man migrated to Europe, to the Caucasus–Black Sea area, to Southeast Asia, to China, and even to America. He did this before the beginning of the last ice cycle of 30,000 BC to 10,000 BC. Where our ancestors spent that long cold winter determined many of the distinguishing characteristics we have today.

Cro-Magnons survived the cold in caves of southern France while ice surrounded them on the north in mid-France on the east in the Alps and on the south in the Pyrenees. For twenty-five thousand years, Cro-Magnon hunted and gathered while he depicted his observations in the paintings of horse and bison he left in the caves. Even more revealing are seasonal compositions he scratched on his bone tools (e.g., spring plants with spawning salmon). Alexander Marshack concluded,[3]

> If Ice Age hunter depicted…different seasons…and if he symbolized these differences with both realistic and abstract images, he probably had words…Thus he was capable of that most symbolic of human functions, speech.

---

3. Alexander Marshack, "Exploring the Mind of Ice-Age Man," *National Geographic* (January 1975).

THE RIGHT HAND OF GOD

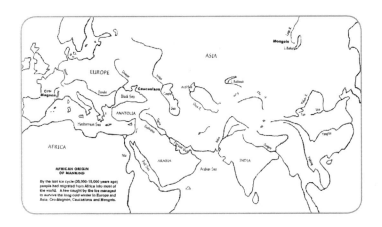

People also survived the ice cycle in the Ukraine–Caucasus region near or in the Black Sea, which was a smaller freshwater lake until seas rose and filled it. Caucasians lost pigment in the skin so that more vitamin D could be assimilated with less sun. On the other hand, extra pigment shields the skin from the sun.

Oriental Mongoloid features developed with the survivors in the Lena River area, almost to Siberia. Since the Siberian ice sheet was thinner than the Euro-American sheets, strong winds scraped the earth bare in areas. The wind and extreme cold caused adaptations to emerge: stocky build, short legs and arms (to minimize frost bite), flat faces, shielded eyes, and coarse straight hair with sparse growth on face and body. After the ice cycle eased, these people moved south and lent their characteristics to most Asians, also to Eskimos in America.[4]

Other groups of people survived the last ice cycle in a world that was vastly different from ours. The Gulf Stream flowed straight across the Atlantic Ocean and showered moisture on North Africa and Asia Minor, where a swath of forest extended. However, a vast amount of water was locked up in snow and ice, so much that the level of the oceans dropped two hundred to

4. Walter A. Fairservis Jr., *The Origins of Oriental Civilization* (The New American Library of World Literature, 1959), 31–32.

three hundred feet. Land was exposed between northeast Asia and Alaska, between Southeast Asia and Australia, also in the Black Sea and Persian Gulf.

Man was poised for the next step, one that added another dimension to his being.

Adam and Eve "Separated" from God

The upper Persian Gulf has been suggested as the location of the Garden of Eden and the Flood. Nothing is certain, but the idea is plausible.

Perhaps the location was the coastal area where the rivers now join and flow as one to the gulf, since silt has filled the area that was flooded. The earlier coastline, ca. 6000 BC, was farther inland than now. At that time, there was more rainfall, and four separate rivers entered the Gulf area. Dr. Jurius Zarins suggested that the rivers of Eden were the Tigris and Euphrates in Iraq and the Gihon or Karun in Iran. The fourth was the Pison or Pishon in Saudi Arabia, which is only a dry riverbed, a *wadi*, that is barely visible now.[5]

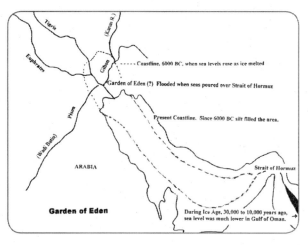

5. Dora Jane Hamblin, "Has the Garden of Eden Been Located at Last?" *Smithsonian* (May 1987). The map of Eden is adapted from her article.

Dr. Zarins traced the stories in the first chapters of Genesis to this area during its nebulous time of prehistory. He included the "rib" story of woman's creation. In Sumerian, *rib* is *ti*, which also means "to make live." Thus, the *lady of the rib* was also the *lady who makes live.* The Sumerian pun did not translate into Hebrew, but the rib story is in the Bible (Genesis 2). And Eve came to symbolize "the mother of all living."

> The man called his wife's name Eve, because she was the mother of all living. (Gen. 3:20, RSV)

In some versions of the Bible, Adam and Eve were not "named" until they ate of the fruit of the Tree of Knowledge of Good and Evil. This is when they *separated* from God and became separate entities, *conscious of self.* But how?

The serpent persuaded the woman to eat and share with the man. One scholar said, "Three cheers for the snake!" God would certainly have wanted them to use the brain He gave them and to have intelligence and knowledge.

Another scholar, Michael Stone[6], pointed out that one sect of Judaism at the time of Christ "regarded the serpent as a positive figure, the wisest of the animals and the instructor of Eve. Eve in turn instructed Adam in the true wisdom." Stone noted that in Aramaic, the words for *Eve, reveal, serpent,* and *beast* are very similar to one another, making possible a play on words that binds the words and ideas together. Satan is not in this version, nor in our biblical version. Satan did not enter the Bible until Job, probably after contact with the Persians. In the Garden of Eden, the serpent represents wisdom, not Satan.

The point is that *before* they ate of the Tree of Knowledge, "generic" man and woman were one with God. They were

---

6. Michael Stone, "Judaism at the Time of Christ," *Scientific American* (January 1973).

unconsciously so much a part of God that they had no concept of self apart from God.[7] When they ate of the Tree of Knowledge—when they *consciously* thought for themselves—they became self-conscious, and their original natural oneness with God was broken.

The Bible stresses man's separation from God. Yet this was actually a good thing *if* Adam and Eve separated in order to know God—to recognize the *other*ness of God while remaining *one* with God through understanding their *same*ness with God. After all, they were created in the image of God. But it was their attitude that ruined the relation. They wanted to be God, to know as much as God, rather than to *know* God Himself. In the Old Testament, to *know* or to *name* meant to be intimately enveloped in the essence of the thing known or named.

After the Fall and separation from God, man began his long, long climb to regain the oneness and harmony he once had with God. The rest of the Bible is the story of how God slowly revealed more and more of Himself as man was able to understand. And God began to bring us back to oneness and intimacy with Him—for us to *consciously* know God.[8]

By the Sweat of the Brow

After Adam and Eve ate of the fruit, they were driven from the Garden. This means they were "driven" from the hunter-gatherer stage. Agriculture began in the upper Tigris area between 8000–7000 BC. When it came down to the Persian Gulf area, the shift to agriculture felt like banishment from Eden.

---

7. Owen Barfield called this "original participation" in his book *Saving the Appearances*.
8. Owen Barfield called this "final participation."

God said, "By the sweat of your brow you shall eat bread" (Gen. 3:19, RSV).

By using their heads, their brains, they would survive. After all, they did eat of the Tree of Knowledge, and with that tasting, the first *unwritten* commandment came into being: *Thou shalt not be stupid*, for the stupidity of the fathers (and mothers) is visited upon the first and second generation, as surely as their iniquity is visited upon the third and fourth generation.

This is *not* in the Bible or the catechism, but you have to admit that children do suffer for their parent's stupidity, as well as the parents themselves. In fact, stupidity just may be the biggest problem in the United States today.

So was using their brains to survive a curse? Or the blessing of God's providence!

Agriculture arrived. Raising grain and animals. Raising Cain and Abel. Cain, a tiller of the soil, represents the shift to agriculture; Abel, the shepherd, the domestication of animals. Both were gigantic steps in cultural evolution, yet both are compressed within phrases in Genesis.[9]

The importance in the biblical story is always the *relation to God*, of Cain and Abel to God, then to each other. Cain was not right with God and slew Abel. A later son, Seth, had the right relation. His descendants called upon the name of the Lord, and through them, God revealed more of Himself.

---

9. *Guns, Germs, and Steel* by Jared Diamond uses more than mere phrases to explain the emergence of agriculture around the world. He said the Tigris–Euphrates area had more small animals and grain grasses to domesticate, so it was the first area into agriculture. It was also first into everything else.

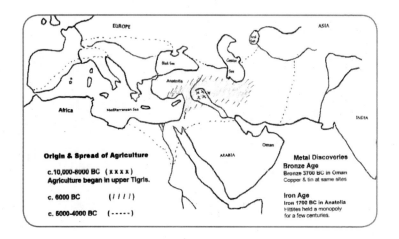

In the meantime, Cain fled to the "east." Susa? Upper Tigris? Lower Anatolia area? Cain had three sons (Gen. 4:20–21, RSV).

1. Jabal was the father of those who live in tents and raise livestock.
2. Jubal was the father of those who play harp and flute.
3. Tubal-Cain was the father of those who forge tools out of bronze and iron.

These were huge steps in social development compressed into phrases.

1. The domestication of cattle, much larger than sheep or goats, was a feat not to be taken lightly. And it never was. The bull remained an important symbol of worship for thousands of years in areas to which it spread. For example, the golden calf in the Medi-East and at Mount Sinai. Cattle in India are still revered. Bullfights in Spain descended from Minoan Crete.
2. A culture of lyre and pipe led to songs and legends of oral history.

3. The forging of bronze and iron acknowledges metalworking as an important step in social development.

Bronze and iron were two different ages two thousand years apart (see agriculture map). Bronze was discovered about 3700 BC by the Sumerians because the copper ore they mined at Oman on the Arabian coast contained tin, so bronze was inevitable. Iron was discovered by Hittites in Anatolia, ca. 1700 BC. Since most of the Old Testament was written about 1200–400 BC, all of these past events were compressed into phrases. The marvel is that the two were recognized as separate achievements.

While Cain's sons furthered cultural development in the east, Seth's sons furthered spiritual development in the west.

Noah "Separated" from Creation

Seth's son Enosh called on the name of the Lord. In the long list of begats, some sons talked with God, and some walked with God. Enoch walked. He was the father of Methuselah, who was the father of Lamech, who was the father of Noah. By then, "sons of God" married daughters of "sons of man," who did not call on the name of the Lord. Things went from bad to worse. God had to do something. He sent the flood—*after* He told Noah to build the ark.

Noah's wife saw the ark in a different light, according to Jeannette Clift George. (She starred as Corrie ten Boom in *The Hiding Place* and started the AD Players in Houston.) She acted out her version of Mrs. Noah. She smoothed her apron and her hair, went outside, and looked around.

> There he is. Still out there on *dry land* building a boat, that he calls an ark. Every cubit is according to instructions from God, so he says. And why? Because God says it is

going to rain. If only it would. But not until he patches that leak in the roof. Day after day they build, while the neighbors—I just can't face them any more. He's got the boys building, too. One of them is bringing in animals—to save from a *flood*. It's so embarrassing. And so hot and muggy. Was that a drop? Is it really going to sprinkle?

The springs of the great deep burst forth and the floodgates of the heavens were opened. And rain fell on the earth forty days and forty nights. (Gen. 7:11–12, NIV)

Dr. Zarins suggested that the flood included water rushing into the Persian Gulf. During the Ice Age, sea levels dropped two hundred to three hundred feet. So sea levels rose with the melting ice and snow. A wall of water suddenly broke through the Straits of Hormuz and inundated the entire Gulf, including the upper Gulf area that is now filled with silt. Dr. Zarins noted that the Sumerians had a legend about coming out of the sea.

We are not sure about a rush of water into the Persian Gulf, but water *did* suddenly flow through the Bosporus Straits into the Black Sea—like a hundred Niagara Falls—and turned the freshwater lake into the salty Black Sea. One theory is that a natural dam at the Bosporus broke during an earthquake, and water flooded in. Another theory is that a huge block of ice—the size of Quebec?—broke off and fell into the North Atlantic.[10] A third theory is that the North American ice sheet weighed sixty-eight thousand trillion tons and depressed the land under ice. The earth bulged up behind the ice cap. As ice melted, land that already bulged up kept rising behind the melted water and trapped it in a huge lake in the Great Lakes–Canada area.

---

10. Harm J. de Blij, geographer and university professor connected with *National Geographic*, said an ice block the size of Quebec slid into the North Atlantic and raised oceans over one hundred feet, ca. 6000 BC.

After more melting, the lake finally broke through an ice dam and emptied into the North Atlantic. A sudden rise in sea level was possibly a worldwide phenomenon and included the Persian Gulf. Other than the deluge, seas rose about a foot a century.

When Noah was back on dry land, he built an altar for a burnt offering. God was pleased and made a covenant with Noah *and* creation, which He sealed with a rainbow. God promised, "Never again will I curse the ground because of man, even though every inclination of his heart is evil from childhood. And never again will I destroy all living creatures" (Gen. 8:21, RSV).

Instead, there was to be a reckoning between men (Gen. 9:6, RSV). "Whoever sheds blood of man, by man shall his blood be shed." Later with Jesus, this became, "With what judgment you judge, you shall be judged. With what measure you mete, it shall be measured to you again" (Matt. 7:1–2). Notice the spiritual evolution between the Old Testament and Jesus in the New Testament.

The significance of the covenant, which God made with Noah *and* creation, was that mankind, society, was *separated* from creation. While creation remains at one with God and obeys God's laws of nature, it still suffers from man's mistreatment. Paul, in Romans 8:19 (RSV), said that creation waits with longing for man's redemption, when man will again be one with God's creation and one with God the Creator, the First Person of the Trinity. This is a big neglect in the church today. We need to reinstate the Creator and have a closer relation to *His* creation.

In the meantime, God promised,

> As long as the earth endures, seedtime and harvest, cold and heat, summer and winter, day and night will never cease. (Gen. 8:22, NIV)

Civilization Began

After the flood, man's actions produced a balance sheet of his own accounting. After all, he ate of the Tree of Knowledge of Good and Evil. Surely he had the sense and good judgment for moral decency. But instead of judging his own actions, he was always more inclined to mete out "justice" and punishment to others. Law and government soon followed in the pre-civ dawning of civilization.

Pre-civ is a new term that must be explained. We cannot jump from the Neolithic Stone Age to civilization. Pre-civ is an important interim stage that began with agriculture and evolved to include everything except writing. With an agri-craft base, pre-civ societies began simple manufacturing, metallurgy, and trading. People were organized for building and irrigation projects. They usually had a remarkable oral tradition in this new dawn of civilization.

Man became so enamored with his dawning of civilization that it was doomed before it started. In the tower-of-Babel story, the people of Shinar (Mesopotamia to the Hebrews) said,

"'Come let us make bricks…Come let us build ourselves a city, with a tower.' And the LORD came down to see the city and the tower which the sons of men had built" (Gen. 11:3–5, RSV).

God was displeased. He confused their language and scattered them over the earth. Again and again, this would happen. It is the leitmotif of the Bible. While the main theme is to *know* God, the recurring theme that wraps around the main theme is the rise and fall of people, nations, and civilizations as man loses closeness to God and His creation. For it is the arrogance with which man builds and worships his city-civilization—which also separates man from God's creation—that dooms civilization to fall (thus the dawn-doom, rise-fall pattern of civ came into being).

After the fall of Babel, people were scattered over the earth. The Babel migrants took their pre-civ ideas with them to lay the foundations for the first round of civilizations. Depending on distance, these were the following:

- ca. 4000 BC Sumerian
- ca. 3500 BC Egyptic and Harappan India
- ca. 3000 BC Minoan in Crete (after sails invented. First sail so far was at Ubaid, near Ur, 3800 BC.)
- ca. 2500 BC Chinese (Hsia legendary period was "pre-civ" on the Wei tributary of Yellow River.)

(The first step temple in Egypt was built of stone hewn to resemble the bricks of a ziggurat. Step temples have been found in Southeast Asia and in the Mayan culture of Mexico. Sumerian-type burials have been found in western China.)

The Babel remnant who remained became the Sumerians. They were first to achieve civilization through *writing*. Perhaps someone picked up a stick and a wet brick to tally the number of bricks laid to build the granary then to tally the baskets of grain delivered to fill the granary. Maybe someone sharpened the stick to make a stylus that was used to press wedge-shaped writing (cuneiform) on to clay tablets. Of all Sumerian tablets discovered so far, 95 percent were commercial.

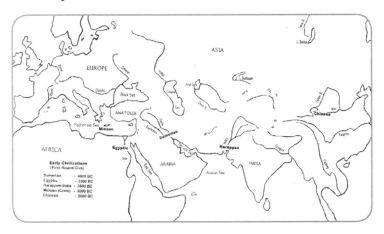

Oral tradition passed on the Babel and flood stories that came to Abraham through Sumerian civilization, as Dr. Zarins pointed out:

> All these early accounts (in the first chapters of Genesis) are linked to Mesopotamia. Abraham indeed is said to have come from Ur, at the time near the (Persian) Gulf, and the writers of Genesis wanted to link up with that history (rather than Egypt though they spent much time in Egypt). So they drew from the literary sources of the greatest civilization that had existed.[11]

The Sumerians were a theocracy that rested on pantheons of gods. Lists of hundreds existed in 2500 BC. River god, sun god, moon god, on and on. Against such a background, ca. 2000 BC, God Almighty revealed to Abraham that He is *one* God of *all* creation—whom we see as God the Creator, the First Person of the Trinity. This was a huge step in religious development that took other people another 1,500 years to reach; some even took 2,500 years.

God Almighty, El Shaddai

Abraham's migration may be seen in relation to other Semitic people. The Arabian Peninsula and North Africa became more arid by 3000 BC as the ice age retreated and the Gulf Stream moved farther north, taking moisture to Europe instead of North Africa and the Middle East. Semitic tribes from the drier Arabian Peninsula migrated into the Sumerian city-states. They migrated before their own stage of oral history had gelled so they absorbed from this earliest civilization, as Abraham did.

---

11. Dora Jane Hamblin, "Has the Garden of Eden Been Located at Last?" *Smithsonian* (May 1987).

They absorbed legends and lore, crafts and agriculture. Ur was the largest city in the world at two square miles in area and forty thousand people.[12] (Population of the world was seven million.) Ur had urban construction, manufacturing, smelting, and dairies. Their shipbuilding led to extensive sailing expeditions. Once sailing vessels from Ur passed through the Straits of Hormuz, Baluchistan, and the Indus Valley were just beyond. Ships hugging the coast developed a brisk trade between the Sumerian city-states and Harappan India. By 2500 bc, the docks at Ur were busy loading and unloading cotton, timber, Indian ivory, gold, copper, lapis lazuli, turquoise.

Around 2000 bc, the trade slowed. Geological shifts at the ports in India interrupted trade. Economic recession followed. Sumerian cities began to decline. The dynamic center of civilization moved from the Persian Gulf toward the Mediterranean. Semitic tribes moved upriver and merged with the existing city-states, especially Babylon, which laid the foundation for Babylonian civilization. Hammurabi, who rose to power in Babylon and sponsored the first written law code, was Semitic. William Foxwell Albright stated that Semitic people moved throughout Mesopotamia and conquered much of it, 2000–1750. The last date is when Hammurabi ruled in Babylon. It became the largest city in the world by 500 bc, when Judah was in exile there.

Abraham was part of the migration from Ur. He was a descendant of Seth according to all of the begats from Adam and Seth to his father Terah (Gen. 11:27–28, rsv):

> Terah was the father of Abram, Nahor and Haran; and Haran was the father of Lot. Haran died before his father Terah in the land of his birth, in Ur of the Chaldeans.

---

12. Ur and Babylon information is from a *Wall Street Journal* review of the Ur-Metropolis exhibit at Pergamon Museum, May 21, 2013.

Terah took Abram, Nahor, and Lot to the land of Haran where Terah died.[13] God told Abram,

> go from your country…kindred…and father's house to the land that I will show you. I will make of you a great nation, and I will bless you, and make your name great, so that you will be a blessing…by you all the families of the earth will be blessed. (Gen. 12:1, RSV)

Abram went, as Soren Kierkegaard explained:[14]

> By faith Abraham went out of the land of his fathers and became a sojourner in the land of promise. He left one thing behind, took one thing with him. He left his earthly understanding behind and took faith with him.

That is, he left civilization behind and took faith with him.

When Abram and Lot passed through Canaan in the vicinity of Shechem, Bethel, and Ai, God said, "To your descendants I will give this land" (Gen. 12:7, RSV).

But Abram and Lot remained nomadic sojourners who went to Egypt to escape famine. When they returned, Lot chose to settle near Sodom while Abram settled in the hinterlands near Hebron. Lot came closer to the evils of civilization while Abram became closer to God. Lot fled when Sodom was destroyed. Although warned not to look back, Lot's wife could not turn her back on the city, so she turned to a pillar of salt (Gen. 19:26, RSV). There is also, or perhaps mainly, a symbolic meaning to the story. She could not turn her back on civilization and met her doom.

Out in the hinterlands, Abraham became closer to God. He had a natural oneness with creation and with the Creator. This

---

13. The area of Haran was probably part of the Ebla culture near Aleppo, which was uncovered in late twentieth century.
14. Soren Kierkegaard, *Fear and Trembling* (New Jersey: Princeton University Press), 31.

became the Hebrew's one-God concept. Instead of the pantheons of nature gods that other people worshipped, Abraham and the early Hebrews saw only *one God of all creation*. William. F. Albright explained that they saw the unity of nature, so there had to be one God sovereign over all creation.[15] Therefore, His name was God Almighty, El Shaddai.

In Genesis 17, God Almighty, El Shaddai, made a covenant with Abram, who was renamed *Abraham* because he would become the father of a multitude of descendants who would possess the land where he sojourned. In return, Abraham, his family, and all his descendants were to be circumcised. This Abraham did. And Sarai became Sarah. But they could not wait for the offspring promised by God. Abraham had a son, Ishmael, by their Egyptian servant Hagar. When Isaac was finally born to Sarah (Gen. 21), Hagar and Ishmael were turned out into the desert.

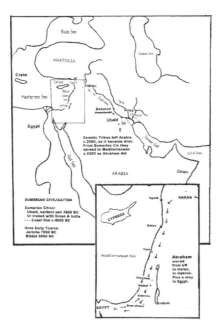

---

15. William Foxwell Albright, *History, Archeology, and Christian Humanism* (New York: McGraw-Hill, 1964), 99.

Ishmael became the father of a nation, the Arabs. The Arabs continued to worship pantheons of gods for the next 2,500 years. In AD 600, Mohammed went back to Father Abraham to found Islam, which has a ritual about Hagar running between two hills pleading to God for help. More on Islam in the proper time slot, AD 600.

In the Ancient Orient are many gods—hundreds are mentioned in the earliest lists from before 2500 BC. William F. Albright observed that in the Old Testament, there is no conflict between the functions of God. He is one God over all, one God of morality and human relation, one God of all nations, one God over all nature. One God supreme, one God who creates man with free will. This change was largely due to the intuitive discovery that the incongruities of polytheism flouted the empirically recognized unity of nature.

Actually, Abraham understood one God over all nature, God the Creator. The rest of this understanding is later Old Testament theology, revealed by God to the Hebrews as they were able to comprehend.

Abraham "Separated" from Society

Isaac was a blessing to Abraham and Sarah. In Genesis 22, God told Abraham to sacrifice Isaac. We might get hung up on the repugnant idea of sacrificing a son. Yet in the context of the times—a period of much appeasing sacrifice, including humans—the test was understandable. Also, we are supposed to look for the deeper message behind the story, which is to put God first, as explained by Soren Kierkegaard in *Fear and Trembling*.

For Abraham, the family or tribe was the ethical, the universal, the highest ideal. When Abraham was asked to sacrifice Isaac, he was asked to rise above this standard, this ethic—above the *ethnic*.

He was asked to rise above family to a prior relation to God, as in Kierkegaard's quotes[16].

> Why then did Abraham do it? For God's sake…because God required this proof of his faith; (and) for his own sake…in order that he might furnish this proof…Duty is precisely the expression for God's will…the individual puts himself in an absolute relation to the absolute—God… Faith is precisely this paradox, that the individual…is higher than the universal…because the individual…stands in an [absolute relation to the absolute—to God—as Abraham did]. It was Abraham's love for Isaac which, by its paradoxical opposition to his love for God that causes his Fear and Trembling and makes the act a sacrifice, an act of faith.

Only now at AD 2000 can we understand what took place 2000 BC. This is what the Reformation was all about. Each person is able to think for himself, choose for himself, of his own free will, that his relation to God will come before anything else in life. Each person experiences a wrestling with God in order to make this choice, in order to make his faith personal and real. This is our one basic choice—on which *all* our other choices depend. The Old Testament is the story of a few who were called and wrestled with *fear and trembling* to put God first. Now all are called—since Pentecost and reaffirmed in the Reformation.

Back to 2000 BC. God made a social covenant with Abraham, which was sealed with a son who would become a tribe, a nation, a spiritual force in the world. The significance of the covenant is that Abraham *separated* his family from the rest of society to further spiritual evolution. They were forbidden to intermarry with other people. They were even separated from other Semitics. This was needed so that Abraham's family could hold on to their

---

16. Kierkegaard, *Fear and Trembling*, 70, 72, 66, 84.

one-God concept as they came into contact with Canaanites and with Baal worship.

Abraham's son Isaac walked easily with God, as every other generation seemed to do. Grandson Jacob, not so easily. After he tricked Esau into selling his birthright, he left in a hurry to go to Haran. In Haran, Jacob married Uncle Laban's daughters, Leah and Rachel, and had eleven of his twelve sons. Benjamin was born near Bethlehem on the way back. Along the way, Jacob had his wrestling-with-God dream after which God renewed His promise to Abraham, now with Jacob. And Jacob was renamed Israel, which means "one who contends with God." He spent an awful long time *contending* before he finally worked in harmony with God.

Jacob's son Joseph walked easily with God. His brothers sold him into slavery in Egypt. He knew they meant it for evil, but God meant it for good. By God's providence, Joseph was in Egypt to provide a haven for his family.

1. A haven from devastating famine—thanks to the grain that Joseph stored during the seven fat years in preparation for the seven lean years of famine.

2. A haven from the battles that surged back and forth in Canaan for centuries while Israel was safe in Egypt. After the Egyptians and Hittites fought themselves to exhaustion, they finally made peace. The last Battle of Kadesh was fought near Haran ca. 1298 BC. By coincidence—or providence—that was about when God called Moses to lead Israel back to Canaan.

3. A haven from outside religious influence. As a separate enclave of foreign people, Israel could hold on to their one-God concept while they grew into a multitude of people. During their four hundred years in Egypt, Israel grew from one tribe to twelve. When their numbers became a threat to the Egyptians and when Joseph was

forgotten, the Hebrews were enslaved to make bricks. Centuries of tediously making bricks is a good time to pause in their history.

Egypt & Hittittes at time of Exodus

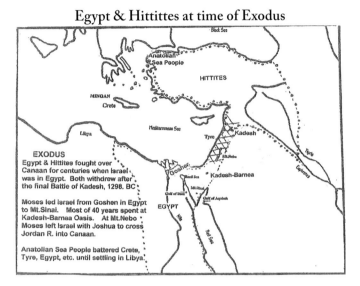

EXODUS
Egypt & Hittites fought over Canaan for centuries when Israel was in Egypt. Both withdrew after the final Battle of Kadesh, 1298. BC

Moses led Israel from Goshen in Egypt to Mt.Sinai. Most of 40 years spent at Kadesh-Barnea Oasis. At Mt.Nebo Moses left Israel with Joshua to cross Jordan R. into Canaan.

Anatolian Sea People battered Crete, Tyre, Egypt, etc. until settling in Libya.

2

Lord, Yahweh, God's Providence

The Spiral of Civilization

During the four centuries the children of Israel were enslaved in Egypt, much was happening in the rest of the world. Before God sent Israel back into that world, He sought to raise their spiritual understanding by revealing His providence in history, starting with His call to Moses.

Of course, God's providence was already at work in prehistory. This was seen when prehistory was correlated with the first chapters of Genesis. Karl Jaspers furthered this correlation in his book *The Origin and Goal of History*.[1]

> Mankind has one single origin and one goal both unknowable in concrete fact but expressed symbolically in Genesis and Apocalypse (Rev). Separate civilizations

---

1. Jaspers 1949 quote was cited by W. Warren Wagar in *The City of Man.*,102

and cultures become only instruments of man's progressive development from his common origin in the remote past to his common destiny in the unforeseeable future.

The scattering of people from the Tower of Babel started the progressive development that Jaspers noted. The rising spiral of civilization, which began when the Babel migrants spread their pre-civ ideas, produced the first round of civilizations in Sumer, Egypt, India, Crete, and China.

The Sumerian and other first round civilizations began to decline with the worldwide recession at the end of the Bronze Age, ca. 2000 BC, when the dynamic center of civilization shifted from the Persian Gulf to the Mediterranean. Also, tribes of Indo-Europeans arrived in horse-drawn carts and chariots. They contributed to the fall then stimulated the rise of the next round of civilizations: Kassite Babylon, Hyksos Egypt, Hittite Anatolia, Vedic India, and Shang China. Indo-Euro tribes also moved into Europe as far as Ireland and produced the Celtic culture of Europe. The ancestors of the Persians circled around from India back to the Susa area.

Who were the Indo-Europeans? They were named for their destinations rather than their place of origin, which was probably north of the Black Sea near the mouths of Danube and Dnieper Rivers. They had a thriving pre-civ with skilled and inventive craftsmen. They invented the wheel and axle for two-wheeled carts and chariots. They tamed the horse and harnessed it to their carts. With these, they swept through two continents. They drove off into the sunrise and sunset when their homeland population spawned an excess number of leaders who needed new domains to rule. (By 3000 BC, Egyptians bred donkeys for pack animals. Around 2000 BC, Indo-Europeans harnessed the horse to two-wheeled carts and chariots. Around 1000 BC, Turks mounted and rode the horse.)

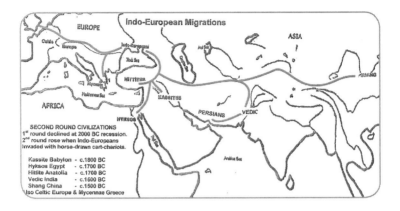

The introduction of horse-cart and chariot technology to awestruck, donkey-pack cultures made it easy for Indo-Euro tribes to establish themselves as rulers atop existing civilizations. Joseph sent donkey carts to bring his family to Egypt so the children of Israel evidently went to Egypt during the Hyksos period, which is also referred to as the time of the shepherd kings. When ex-shepherd Joseph was forgotten and when the children of Israel became so numerous they were a threat to Egypt, they were enslaved to make bricks. Slavery and oppression have a way of uniting people—until it becomes too oppressive. That was when God called Moses to deliver them.

"I Am" Called Moses

God appeared to Moses in the burning bush. God said, "Come, I will send you to Pharaoh that you may bring forth my people, the sons of Israel, out of Egypt."

Moses debated with God.[2]

Moses: Who am I to do this?

God: I will be with you.

Moses: Who will I say has sent me?

---

2.   Excerpts from Exodus 3:11–14, RSV.

God: I Am Who I Am. Say this to the people of Israel, "I Am has sent me to you. This is my name forever."

God explained to Moses,

> I am the lord, I appeared to Abraham, to Isaac, and to Jacob, as God Almighty (El Shaddai) but by my name the lord I did not make myself known to them. (Exod. 6:3, RSV)

LORD in all capital letters is YHWH or JHVH—with vowels, Yahweh or Jehovah. But vowels were a long way off. In the meantime, the four letters of the Tetragrammaton were never spoken. (*Tetra* means "four." *Grammaton* means "letters," from the same root word as *grammar*.) The Hebrews later substituted *Elohim* or read the word as *Adonai*, which is *Lord* with capital *L* and *ord* in small letters.

YHWH is related to the verb *to be* and also suggests *to breathe*, as Owen Barfield explained.[3]

> The Hebrew word for "Jew" may similarly be rendered YHWDI; the texture of the language hints that a devout Jew could hardly name his race without tending to utter the Tetragrammaton...(But they did not speak the word for)...no being who speaks through his throat can call a wholly other and outer Being "I."

God explained to Moses who He was, then God continued,

> I also established my covenant with them, (with Abraham, Isaac, Jacob) to give them the land of Canaan, the land in which they dwelt as sojourners...Say to the people of Israel, "I will redeem you with an *outstretched arm* and with great acts of judgment.' (Exod. 6:4, 6, RSV)

---

3. Barfield, *Saving the Appearances*, 113-114.

The outstretched arm of God, His right hand, is the providence of God. This is what God now revealed to the Hebrews. He is sovereign over all nations as well as all creation.

Moses went to Pharaoh. Each time Moses said, "Let my people go," Pharaoh said no. So God sent a plague. Each was designed to undercut some facet of Egyptian religion, which undermined Pharaoh and showed that God is sovereign over all creation. Finally, Passover. The angel of death *passed over* Hebrew houses marked with lamb's blood while death struck down the firstborn in Egyptian houses. Israelites escaped through the Reed Sea, on the Gulf of Suez near the land of Goshen. By God's providence, by His outstretched arm, Moses led them out of Egypt.

At Mount Sinai, God gave Moses the Ten Commandments, which were needed for *judgment*. The first four commandments instructed the Hebrews in their relation to God; the other six, in their relation to one another. Since the relation to God is the foundation of religion—and of everything else—that relation had to be clearly defined. The LORD your God is *one* God. You shall have *no* other gods before Him. No graven images. No icons. No representations of God's creation. No pictures of sun, moon, cattle, nor anything else—lest they worship the image and fail to look beyond to God. Nothing was to come between them and God.

The "I Am" concept was given to Moses because I Am is an abstract idea that allows unlimited depth of meaning as God continued to reveal more and more of Himself. Now, during the Exodus, the important dawning revelation was God's providence in history.

Israel saw that God led them with a cloud by day and a pillar of fire by night. God provided manna each morning for food. God provided stone tablets with the Ten Commandments so they could live together in harmony. Moses led the people in the Sinai covenant to uphold the Ten Commandments. He sealed the covenant with animal sacrifices then threw blood on the altar and on the people while he said, "Behold the blood of the covenant the LORD has made with you" (Exod. 24:8, RSV).

God provided Moses with instructions for the Ark of the Covenant, a chest to hold the tablets of the covenant and some of the manna. The top of the lid remained empty, for it was the seat of the Lord, who was not to be depicted, although there was a seraph at each end of the lid. God also gave Moses specific instructions for building a tent tabernacle.

Both the tabernacle and the ark were easily transported during their forty years of wandering. Whenever they stopped, each tribe had an assigned duty in erecting the tabernacle and an assigned place to camp around it. The duties of the priesthood were given to the Levites. Moses recorded these instructions from God in the parts of Genesis, Exodus, Leviticus, Numbers, and Deuteronomy, which he wrote at the Kadesh–Barnea oasis where Israel spent most of the forty years. Debate exists about Moses writing any of the Pentateuch. Maybe most was oral, but Moses probably wrote parts of the Pentateuch. Moses was schooled in Pharaoh's court, where they had a hieratic script in addition to hieroglyphs. The Hebrews also had writing of a sort.

God stretched out his hand to Israel. He provided for their needs. All they had to do was to take His hand as He led them and to *remember* what He did for them—the blessings of His providence—as they revered His name, the LORD, I Am.[4]

---

4. As stated above, "I Am" allows unlimited depth of meaning and is the same as "God Is." But we seldom leave it at that. We add some limiting predicate adjective or nominative. The favorite is "God is love." But that leaves out any concept of the Creator, of God's providence in history, and of His Holy Spirit. It omits the Trinity.

God's Providence

It was no accident that God led Israel out of Egypt while the sea people battered the coast. It was no accident that God led them through forty years in the wilderness while their Creator concept was reinforced and while God prepared the most opportune time for them to enter and claim the Promised Land. But all the while, they murmured and doubted God's providence. After all, they spent forty years in the desert with only crumbs of manna when they expected to be in the Land of Milk and Honey.

Again and again, God reminded Israel, "I am the LORD your God, who brought you out of the land of Egypt, out of bondage." Through such reminders, God emphasized His providence in history. Since they had no word for history, the Hebrews simply recited the whole litany of events by which God led them during the Exodus. This is history in its most literal, graphic sense. Also a dramatic way to remember it!

In time, Israel developed a unique sense of time and history that was ongoing and purposeful, in contrast to other people who saw endless repeating cycles with no purpose (this idea is from William Foxwell Albright). God gave this unique sense of history to the Hebrews. By the time He invested a couple of thousand years in them, He could not give up on them—no matter how stiff-necked they were (and they were stiff-necked)—because no one else reached back to the dawn of history the way they did. And no one else came in contact with the dominant civilizations of man's rising spiral of development the way God led the ragtag Hebrews from early Sumer to Egypt then back to Canaan.

It was no accident that God led Israel back to Canaan when He did—*after* the Egyptian and Hittite superpowers battled themselves to exhaustion and withdrew from the area and *before* the Assyrians rose to become the next superpower to conquer the area. Between superpowers was the only time small nations could exist.

Who were the Hittites? Until fairly recent archeological discoveries, the Hittites were considered a negligible group of tribes who were overly magnified in the Bible because of Israel's own small size. But the Hittites, in the ore-rich mountains of Anatolia, discovered the use of iron (ca. 1750 BC) and ushered in the Iron Age. They held a monopoly on iron production for years. This helped account for their strength on a par with Egypt.

The Hittites and Egyptians made a battleground of Canaan while the Hebrews were sheltered in Egypt. The Hittites also battled and conquered territory downriver on the Tigris and Euphrates, almost to the Persian Gulf. Their last conquest on the Tigris was a native tribe of Assyrians. After centuries of war and the final Battle of Kadesh in 1298 BC, the two exhausted superpowers, Egypt and Hittites, finally made peace and withdrew from Canaan, as did the Hittites from the Tigris area.

It was no accident that Moses was called about 1290 BC to lead his people out of Egypt. About that same time, Anatolian sea people raided the east Mediterranean. First, the sea people raided neighboring Hittites on Anatolia, then Crete, Tyre, and Egypt. As one historian noted, even Rameses was hard-pressed to keep *in* the Hebrews and to keep *out* the sea people at the same time. So the Hebrews slipped out by way of the Reed Sea while the sea people battered the coast and finally settled in Libya.

Not too many years later, Libyans became the ruling dynasty in Egypt, which was ruled by foreign dynasties until World War I in AD 1918. Superpowers battling to exhaustion may provide a lesson for all time.

Interim of Small Nations

When the second round civilizations declined, especially when Egyptian and Hittite superpowers withdrew from Canaan, small nations filled the power vacuum. Israel was one of many small nations in the Canaan–Anatolia area around 1000 BC. Others were Lydia, Aram, Phoenicia, and emerging Assyria.

Lydia, with its capital at Sardis, reaped the benefit of the ore-rich mountains of Anatolia as the Hittites had. But Lydian kings mined *gold*, not iron. Their kings became symbols of wealth. *Midas touch*, for the king whose touch turned everything to gold, even his daughter, and *rich as Croesus* are phrases still in use today. Lydians added the minting of coins to mankind's treasury of innovations.

Aram (Syria) has been centered around Damascus and the caravan trade since 1500 BC. Although Aram was one of the first nations to fall to the Assyrians, the Aramaic people continued to flourish because the Assyrians left commerce in their hands. Their Aramaic language, which Christ spoke, survived for hundreds of years. Perhaps this illustrates the lasting influence of commerce compared to conquests of the sword.

Assyrians were a native group located on the Tigris who managed to survive Hittite domination and to defend themselves against other groups in the area. Around 750, they suddenly became aggressive. They introduced mounted cavalry and more brutality to war, plus roads, a postal system, and provincial government. All of these suggest contact with China and the Chou Dynasty (1125–249 BC), which was taken over by Turks who rode in on their horses and ruled as titular head of the Chou, 1027–770 BC. When the Turks were ousted, they swept down and set themselves up as rulers over the Assyrians. The exit of Turks in 770 BC meshes with the aggressive rise of Assyria and conquest of Israel in 722 BC—with fifty years for them to become established.

As the Chou Dynasty declined, ca. 500 BC, China fell into warring states. Confucius tried to hold it together with a uniting history, but the first ruler of the Ch'in (or Qin) Dynasty burned the books then claimed he was the first emperor of a dynasty that would never end. He took mercury for a longer life, slept in a different palace each night to escape assassins, and built his memorial grave with hundreds of life-size figures, which were discovered in late twentieth century. When the mercury elixir worked its charms and the emperor was on his deathbed, he sent a message to his son working on the Great Wall to come home and take over. The messengers rewrote the message, and the son was either killed or killed himself in obedience to his father's purported message. So the Ch'in Dynasty lasted all of fourteen years, 221–207 BC.

Canaanites in the coastal city-states of Ugarit, Byblos, Sidon, and Tyre were known by the names of their cities rather than by the cedars of Lebanon or by the name of the purple dye they manufactured from shells. From this purple dye, the Greeks derived the name *Phoenicia*, which they gave to the cities. Phoenicians were at their peak during the interim between Hittite and Assyrian domination, 1200–800 BC. The oldest city, Byblos, began as a fishing village, ca. 5000 BC, and gave its name to the Bible, to bibliographies, and to European libraries—*Bibliothek*. The Phoenicians invented a simplified phonetic alphabet that was probably devised out of necessity in order to record their trade contracts with many different people (*phonetic* is from *Phoenician*).

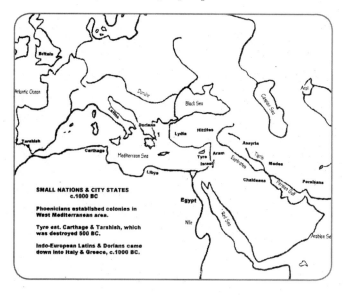

SMALL NATIONS & CITY STATES
c.1000 BC

Phoenicians established colonies in West Mediterranean area.

Tyre est. Carthage & Tarshish, which was destroyed 500 BC.

Indo-European Latins & Dorians came down into Italy & Greece, c.1000 BC.

Phoenician cities established colonies in the west Mediterranean: Tyre founded Carthage on the Tunisian peninsula in order to control passage between the east and west Mediterranean Sea. Tyre also established Tarshish, a sister colony to Carthage and its biggest rival. Tarshish was located on the Guadalquivir River on the southwest coast of Spain in order to control passage between the Mediterranean and the Atlantic. Tarshish built strong ships to sail in the Atlantic. These ships were the ones Solomon had copied for his fleet, which was built by craftsmen of Tyre.

After parent cities in the east Mediterranean fell to the Assyrians, the western colonies continued their extensive seafaring and commerce. Carthage manufactured purple dye, textiles, glass, and metal. Their tin came from Britain. In order to secure its Atlantic trade routes, Carthage plotted the destruction of Tarshish ca. 500 BC. Carthage then became and remained the dominant power in the western Mediterranean until Romans defeated them in three Punic Wars. After the third war, Carthage was destroyed ca. 150 BC, about a century and a half before Christ.

Yet for one thousand years, maritime Phoenicians took Baal or Bel with them every place they voyaged: first to the west Mediterranean and the west coast of Spain, then to Celts in Europe and Scandinavia. Perhaps even to North America.

So here were the Phoenicians spreading Baal all over the world, long before and long after the Hebrew trek to Egypt. Was God really in control of history? Indeed He was, for in time—God's time—Phoenician Astarte became Viking Eostre, and finally, Christian Easter.

In the meantime, the Hebrews made their trek back to Canaan.

The Promised Land

Moses knew he would not enter Canaan because he disobeyed God when he smote the rock for water. He led the children of Israel to Mount Nebo in Moab in readiness to cross the Jordan River near Jericho. There, Moses gave his farewell speeches recorded in Deuteronomy.

He then led the people in the Deuteronomic covenant to prepare them for life in Israel. In the Deutero covenant, obedience to the commandments was linked to love, reinforced by the blessings of obedience *or* the curses of consequences. Seven versions of the following passage appear in Deuteronomy.

> The LORD our God is one LORD; love the Lord your God with all your heart, with all your soul and with all your might. (Deut. 6:4–5, RSV)

In Deuteronomy 11:2 (NIV), Moses explained,

> Remember that your children were not the ones who saw and experienced the discipline of the LORD your God; His majesty, His mighty hand, His outstretched arm.

Moses then recited the acts of God that brought Israel out of Egypt as he instructed the people, "Teach them to your children. Talk about them when you sit, walk, wake, and go to sleep."

Thus, Moses completed the "call" he received from I Am at the burning bush. He passed his staff to loyal Joshua, who waited partway up Mount Sinai while Moses was given the tablets with the Ten Commandments. Joshua and Caleb were the only people who left Egypt and experienced the entire Exodus. They were two of the twelve spies sent into Canaan to assess the situation. Only, they were ready to go on in, for the Lord was with them. The other ten feared to enter and exaggerated the size of the enemy. So entry was postponed a few more decades.

Finally, all was ready. Moses passed his staff to Joshua and went up Mount Nebo to view the land God had promised to Abraham, Isaac, Jacob. Moses died in peace. Israel grieved for thirty days.

God led Joshua through the parted waters of the Jordan and the conquest of Canaan. After Joshua "fit the battle of Jericho" Israel avoided city strongholds and mainly conquered the countryside. Joshua then divided the land among the twelve tribes as God instructed him. The Levites received no land since they were the priestly tribe. Joseph's two sons, Ephraim and Manasseh, were treated as separate tribes to make up the twelve. Finally, the land was fairly secure against their enemies.

By then, Joshua was old and ready for his own farewell. Joshua called the elders, leaders, and judges of the twelve tribes to Shechem, where Israel gathered for festivals (Passover in spring, harvest in fall). The priests brought the ark throne of God before the people. Joshua renewed their covenant with God. First, he proclaimed the law of God as written in the book of Moses. Next, he recited the mighty acts of God that he traced back to Abraham in the past, through the Exodus, on to the present conquest of Canaan. Thus, he expanded their view of history.

Joshua said, "But as for me and my household, we will to serve the LORD." The people joined in and agreed to keep God's covenant (Josh. 24:15, NIV).

During Israel's two hundred years of Judges, 1220–1020 BC, the twelve tribes were not united unless an outside threat caused a hero to rise. Judges such as Gideon saved Israel, but the Hebrews wanted a king like other nations. The high priest Samuel cautioned against a king, for God was their king. Finally, he anointed Saul of the tribe of Benjamin to be the first king of Israel. During Saul's reign, the Philistines took the ark from Shiloh, the center of worship, when Samuel was priest. Saul did not seek its return, and he gradually fell away from God.

God told Samuel to anoint a son of Jesse from the tribe of Judah as Saul's successor. Samuel looked over the sons Jesse brought to him then asked if there was another son. David was called from herding the sheep. Samuel anointed him. David returned to his sheep. When he took food to his brothers battling the Philistines, he agreed to fight Goliath. He felled the giant with a stone from his slingshot then cut off Goliath's head with a sword.

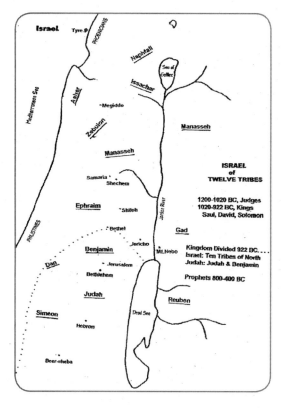

David was called to play music to soothe Saul. David and Saul's son Jonathan became close friends. All three went to battle the enemies of Israel. People began to sing, "Saul has slain his thousands, and David, his tens of thousands." Saul was jealous and tried to kill David, pursuing him like a fugitive. David did not avenge himself. He had two opportunities to do so, but he left vengeance to the Lord.

After Saul's death, the twelve tribes sent elders to Hebron where David was already king of Judah. (Hebron was the area that Abraham chose when he separated from Lot. When Sarah died, Abraham bought a burial plot where she and many of the patriarchs were buried.) The twelve tribes made a pact of confederation with David and made him king of all Israel. David ruled from Hebron for seven years, then from Jerusalem for thirty-three years.

David captured Jerusalem from the Jebusites. The city had been bypassed during the conquest. Since Jerusalem was not part of any tribe, it made an ideal new capital and center of worship. David chose the site for the temple on adjacent Mount Moriah, which he purchased from a Jebusite who used the flat rock for a threshing floor (by tradition, this was the place where Abraham planned to sacrifice Isaac). After David recovered the Ark of the Covenant from the Philistines, he put it in a tent tabernacle on Mount Moriah.

After a while, David noticed, "Here I am living in a palace of cedar, while the Ark of the Covenant of the LORD is under a tent" (1 Chron. 17:1, NIV). David decided to build a temple. But Nathan, Samuel's successor and spiritual advisor to David, explained that David was not to build the temple.

Actually, God was quite satisfied with the tent. God asked, "Did I ever say, 'Why have you not built me a house of cedar'" (1 Chron. 17:6, NIV).

God explained that He took David from his flocks in the pasture and made him ruler of His people. God will do even more. He will build a "house" for David through a son, who is the one who shall build a house for God.

> I will be his father and he will be my son…I will set him
> over my house and my kingdom forever; his throne will be
> established forever. (1 Chron. 17:13-14, NIV)

This refers to Jesus, but David did not understand. So he went ahead with his extensive preparations for the temple his son Solomon was to build. David amassed a hundred talents of gold, a million talents of silver, bronze, and iron too great to be weighed, also cedar and stone, plus craftsmen of every skill, to build the temple (1 Chron. 22:14, NIV).

David represented the peak of Israel's glory—to which Israel always tried to return, even today. It was a golden age when much of the Old Testament was written. David contributed many psalms. His mentor priests, Samuel, Nathan, and Gad, kept records that were used to write Samuel, Kings, and Chronicles. Solomon added Song of Solomon in his youth, Proverbs in his years of wisdom, and the musings of Ecclesiastes in his old age.

In the meantime, Solomon offered thousands of sacrifices, especially at the temple dedication. Just imagine! Two thousand cattle! One hundred and twenty thousand sheep and goats!

Solomon ushered in the extravagance and arrogance that brought decline. One historian described Solomon's reign as that of "a pastoral people trying to put on the trappings of Oriental splendor." During Israel's forty years of wandering in the desert, the Hebrews were reduced to the pastoral reality of down-to-earth existence and dependence on God. Even manna from heaven! How soon they forgot God's providence.

Solomon certainly did. He built cities, including chariot cities such as Megiddo, with much forced labor from the tribes. He hired Hiram of Tyre to build the temple and to build a fleet of ships modeled on the ships of Tarshish so he could sail out the Gulf of Aqaba and the Red Sea to trade with Sheba at the end of the Arabian Peninsula and with Ophir (India?). In the process of his trade negotiations, Solomon collected a harem of seven hundred wives and three hundred concubines. Few left their pagan religions. No wonder the nation became estranged from God.

After Solomon died in 922 BC, the nation divided. The confederation pact of the twelve tribes was not renewed with Solomon's successor, Rheoboam. Jeroboam, who had supplied forced labor from the tribes of Ephraim and Manasseh, wanted assurances from Rheoboam that the demands for forced labor would be reduced. Older advisors urged Rheoboam to agree. After all, everything was built by then. Younger advisors said no. Rheoboam took their advice and refused to yield. So the ten tribes in the north separated from Judah and Benjamin in the south.

Jerusalem, the center of worship and sacrifice, was located in Judah. This made access to the temple difficult for the north. Omri, king of Israel sixty years after Solomon (865 BC), captured Samaria to make it the capital and center of worship in the north. Omri's son Ahab married Jezebel, a princess of Tyre. She continued her Baal worship. Israel became ever more estranged from God. God sent prophets to bring them back.

Prophets Foretell Israel's Fall

Prophets used highly dramatic means to make their point. When Ahab built altars to Baal for Jezebal, Elijah wandered into Ahab's court and announced that it would not rain until Yahweh commanded it. After three years of drought, Elijah returned. He proposed a contest with the priests of Baal to see who could ignite a stack of wood—drenched in water—and make it rain. Losers to be executed! The Baal priests failed. God ignited Elijah's wood, and the rains came. Elijah killed the Baal priests then fled when Jezebel tried to kill him.

While in the wilderness, Elijah learned that God no longer spoke in the earthquake, burning bush, or whirlwind (1 Kings 19:11–12, NIV). Not through outward signs but through a still small voice. Owen Barfield saw this as the indwelling of God's Spirit, an important step in religious development.

Elisha succeeded Elijah. Both prophets showed that Yahweh, not Baal, gives life and controls nature. They affirmed God the Creator, the First Person of the Trinity. Neither wrote books of the Bible. The rest of the prophets, who wrote books of the Bible, emphasized morality—living a life of righteousness through the indwelling Spirit of God. God is righteous and demands righteousness of his people, even "chosen" Israel, or judgment will come.

God gave new insight through the prophets:

> I despise your feasts...solemn assemblies...burnt offerings...I will not accept them...But let justice roll down like waters and righteousness like an ever-flowing stream.[5] (Amos 5:21–24, RSV)

> I desire 'hesed' [steadfast love, loyalty] not sacrifice; the knowledge of God, rather than burnt offerings. (Hosea 6:6, RSV)

Hosea bought back his unfaithful wife to show how forgiving God was of Israel's unfaithfulness. God forgives but still wants *hesed* and the knowledge of God.

Micah was from a rural area, so he thought all evil resided in the cities, especially Samaria and Jerusalem, which were overdue for God's judgment. "Jerusalem shall become a heap of ruins, and the mountain of the house a wooded height" (Mic. 3:12, RSV). Micah said the temple will be destroyed, yet in his next breath, he said that their religion will be the highest religion.

> The mountain of the house of the LORD shall be established as the highest of the mountains...and many nations shall come and say: "Come, let us go up to the mountain of the LORD, to the house of the God of Jacob; that he may teach us His ways and we may walk in His paths." For out of Zion shall go forth the law and the word of the LORD from Jerusalem. He shall judge between peoples and nations

---

5. Martin Luther King used this passage in his speeches.

afar off…and they shall beat their swords into plowshares and spears into pruning hooks.[6] (Mic. 4:1–3, RSV)

Micah 5:2 (RSV) prophesied that out of Bethlehem is to come "one who is to be ruler in Israel, whose origin is from old, from ancient days." That is, his origin goes back to Abraham, even to the origin of mankind, as Christ's did, the son of all mankind.

The prophets spoke in vain. By the time they finished prophesying, the northern kingdom of Israel (Samaria) fell to the Assyrians, 722 BC. The ten tribes of the north vanished from history. Some were deported. Others intermarried to become the despised half-breed Samaritans. Many migrated to Judah, taking their emphasis on Deuteronomy with them. Thanks to King Hezekiah, Judah remained a semi-independent tribute-paying kingdom under the Assyrians.

A century after the fall of Israel, prophet Zephaniah prompted a few reforms in Judah under King Josiah, 621 BC. The temple was cleaned; a scroll was found. Wonder of wonders! A part of Deuteronomy! The scroll was read to the people. Josiah and all of Judah renewed the Deutero covenant to walk with the Lord and to keep his commandments (2 Kings 23:3). Passover was celebrated as it had not been since Samuel. The country was cleansed of false gods, altars, mediums, and wizards.

Barely were the reforms in place when Josiah rode to battle at Megiddo, the chariot city of Solomon. Pharaoh Neco of Egypt was on his way through Judah to help Assyria against the allied Medes, Scythians, and Chaldeans. Josiah tried to stop Neco. He was shot with an arrow and taken back to Jerusalem in a chariot. He died 609 BC. Neco went on to join the Assyrians in defeat at the Battle of Carchemish, 606 BC. The victorious Medes returned to the east and merged with the Persians. The Scythians went to Europe and India. The Chaldeans remained as rulers in Babylon.

---

6.   Isaiah 2:2–4 echoed Micah in this.

Habakkuk saw the Chaldeans as a new threat to Judah. He knew God was in control of history. Judah deserved judgment and punishment, but why should it be ladled out by a nation more evil than they? Still Habakkuk urged the people to keep the faith and the covenant. "The LORD is in His holy temple" (Hab. 2:20, RSV).

Jeremiah also saw the threat from Chaldean Babylon. He felt the reforms of Josiah were superficial, with too much emphasis on the temple and Jerusalem and the idea that neither would ever fall. Inviolable Jerusalem! But Yahweh was greater than Jerusalem *or* the temple and could do just fine without either.

People needed a change of heart, where sin was rooted. They needed to "circumcise their hearts."

> Behold, the days are coming says the LORD, when I will make a new covenant with the house of Israel and Judah…I will put my law within them, and I will write it upon their hearts and I will be their God, and they shall be my people. (Jer. 31:31, 33, RSV)

Judah rejected Jeremiah's prophecy—and rejected Jeremiah himself. They put him in a dry cistern to die—a rather apt punishment since he said their religion was like a dry cistern. Jeremiah was rescued and finally exiled to Egypt.

Prophets of Judah's Exile

Jeremiah knew whereof he spoke. Just after the turn of the century at 600 BC, Chaldeans took the cream of Judah to Babylon. Judah rebelled a decade later. The Chaldeans destroyed the temple and deported all but the very lowest Hebrews.

Ezekial came with the "cream" and got his call in Babylon. He helped priests edit and save the books of the Old Testament that they brought with them. Synagogues were started to teach the books and the traditions of the faith so Hebrews could exist as a people of faith—even without a country.

Ezekial had a vision of Yahweh's throne transported on wheels, which went in every direction. Yahweh was *not* destroyed when Judah fell. God was not confined to Jerusalem or the temple or the geographic area of Judah. He was Lord of all creation—in every direction those wheels could go. He was even with the exiles in faraway foreign Babylon.

This was a completely new idea. People of that time believed each nation had its own god who looked after his people in his territory. But Yahweh was *universal*. He was with them in Babylon and would restore them to Judah. Ezekial saw this in his vision of the valley of dry bones. When the spirit of God moved over the bones (leg bone connected to the thigh bone, thigh bone to the hip bone), they were all reconnected, covered with flesh and lived again (Ezek. 37).

Second Isaiah of chapters 40–66 had the same message. This Isaiah was called by God to "comfort, comfort my people" weeping in Babylon. Assure them of the magnitude of the Lord, who is sovereign over all creation and sovereign over all nations, of all history. He will set the captives free.

To God, oceans are handfuls, islands are dust, nations are drops. "After all," asks God,

Who stirred up one from the east [Cyrus of Persia] whom victory meets at every step? Who has performed and done this, called the generations from the beginning? [of history? Of mankind?] (Isa. 41:2, 4, RSV)

I, the LORD who says to Cyrus, "He is my shepherd, and he shall fulfill all my purpose", saying of Jerusalem, "She shall be built" and of the temple, "Your foundation shall be laid." Thus says the LORD to his anointed, to Cyrus, whose right hand I have grasped. (Isa. 44:28–45:1, RSV)

God will restore the people and the temple in Judah through Cyrus, whom God has anointed to further God's purpose, to further God's providence—*but*, God told Isaiah,

It is too light a thing…that Israel be restored for its own sake. They are to be a light to all nations so God's salvation may reach to the end of the earth. (Isa. 49:6)

Isaiah said the foundation of the new Jerusalem will be as if it were gem-studded because it will be established in righteousness with all sons taught by the Lord—with God's spirit in each person, not just speaking to prophets as of old (Isa. 54 :12–13, RSV).

Joel had the same message. "And it shall come to pass afterward, that I will pour out my spirit on all flesh" (Joel 2:28, REV). This was fulfilled at Pentecost.

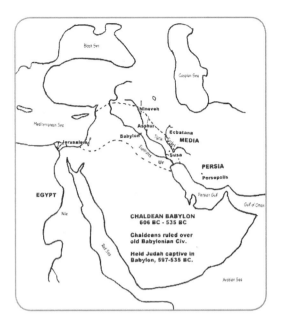

In Isaiah 55, God invited everyone to eat and drink of the Spirit, the real food, the free food, so their souls may live. God's covenant with David will be fulfilled. David's son, the new David, God's Messiah (Jesus), will call all nations to the house of the Lord of Israel.

> Seek the LORD and his righteousness for God's ways and thoughts are higher than man's. For as the rain and snow come down from heaven, and return not thither but water the earth making it bring forth and sprout...so shall my word be that goes forth from my mouth; it shall not return to me empty, but it shall accomplish that which I purpose. (Isa. 55:10–11, RSV)

God's Word will accomplish God's purpose. His Word will bring the spiritual kingdom of God to earth. And all people will *know* God—intimately.

Israel is to go forth in joy and peace! And creation will join in singing! Arise, shine for your light has come…And nations shall come to your light. (Isa. 60:1, 3, RSV)

I am coming to gather all nations and tongues and they shall come and see my glory…to my holy mountain…all flesh shall come to worship before me, says the LORD. (Isa. 66:18, 20, 23)

The Jews (for they became Jews in Babylon) were to return and tell all nations about their God, the Lord, who was sovereign in history and used Cyrus of a foreign nation to restore Judah. God was preparing the world for their message.

Religion in the Air as Pantheons Crumble

Pantheons of gods began to crumble in civilizations all over the world as people looked for more religious depth. They wanted more than nature gods of the sun and moon, more than gods with the capricious morals of humans.

According to Karl Jaspers, religion was in the air between 800–200 BC when the first universal traditions in religion and philosophy were created in China, India, the Near East, and Greece. Actually, the first universal religion started with Abraham over 1,500 years before this. The Old Testament prophets fit into this time slot and need to be seen in the context of this period of religious development, which was unfolding in other areas.

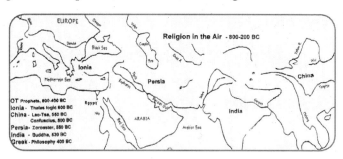

China

The Chou Empire, 1122–49 BC, spread in a wedge from the Wei River to the coast between the Yellow and Yangtze Rivers. Turks set themselves up as rulers for two centuries until they were ousted about 770 BC (some went to Assyria). Two centuries later, the Chou Dynasty began to decline, and China fell into warring states. About 500 BC, Confucius tried to hold China together. He compiled a unified history of China and instituted civil-service exams. He applied empirical logic to religion and urged morality because it was tied to cosmic unity.

Lao-Tse also saw a lack of values in their disintegrating society. He founded Taoism, which urged a return to nature and the way (Tao) of the universe rather than man-made civilization, which caused the lack of values, corruption, and social irresponsibility that plagued China. Confucius and Lao-Tse realized that people needed to maintain their relation to God's creation for social soundness. They recognized the First Person of the Trinity.

India

The many people who invaded India merely added their layer on top of existing culture and civilization (partly the reason for the castes). Harappan culture (which traded with Sumerians) was overlaid with the Vedic of the Indo-Europeans and that by Hinduism. In time, the Hindu rituals of the Brahman priesthood became more important than God. Upanishad writers sought a single reality behind the many gods and also sought union with that spiritual reality as man's chief end. They did not believe that the world was real, but was an illusion. The bond with earth had to be severed by reaching a point of no desire. Buddha, 530 BC, urged enlightenment and Nirvana through complete denial of self, family, and the world. They saw Spirit, Third Person of the Trinity.

Ancient Greece

Anatolian peasants took their sheep, goat, grain, grape, and olive culture to the Greek mainland ca. 4000 BC. By 2500 BC, they had fortified towns with paved streets and storm sewers (as in Harappan India, Crete, and Etruscan Italy). They also had columned great halls with a central fireplace and wall murals. Indo-Euro tribes, ca. 2000 BC, added their language, sky-god and brotherhood concepts, plus horse and chariot, warriors, minstrels, and beaker-wielding tribal chiefs in hilltop forts. They kept the columned great halls, but the murals changed.

By 1600 BC, Mycenae (Indo-Euros at the isthmus of Corinth) became the most important citadel-kingdom because of their trade with Hittites, Egyptians, Minoan Crete, and Phoenician cities. Mycenae followed the Minoan and Phoenician lead by adopting much of their culture and by establishing colonies in the Mediterranean.[7] Mycenae inherited the Minoan colonies after earthquakes and tidal waves disabled the Minoans. But they were too weak a sea power to maintain the colonies or to contain the Anatolian sea people as Minoan Crete had. Mycenaens were weakened by the piracy of the sea people and by the Trojan War, which was fought to protect breadlines to their Black Sea granary as much as Helen's pretty face. They finally succumbed to invading Dorians, who easily conquered Hellas with their iron weapons ca. 1125 BC. Many refugees fled to Ionia on the Anatolian coast.

Assimilation of the Dorians caused a dark age in Hellas. In the midst of it, ca. 800 BC, Homer yearned for the Mycenaen age

---

7. William F. Albright, *History, Archeology, and Christian Humanism*, 270. We now know that the material culture of Phoenicia, Cyprus, Anatolia, and the Aegean was thoroughly syncretized during the seventh and sixth century BC, following several centuries of interpenetration of Aegean and Phoenician civilization. Hellenes already borrowed much of their art and architecture, plus the alphabet.

in his *Iliad* and *Odyssey*. But a greater age was dawning, led by Ionia around 600 BC.[8] Ionia's main contribution was Thales's use of abstract terms in geometry. This laid the foundation for formal logic that produced philosophy and replaced the pantheons of gods during the classic period. But Persia had to be defeated first.

Persia

During the reign of Cyrus, ca. 550 BC, Zoroaster (or Zarathustra) evolved an ethical religion that was rather abstract and made the Magi superfluous. Ahura Mazda, the spirit of light and good, created the world through virtues such as justice, truth, right living, and integrity. People were to live in harmony with these. But it was not easy. Ahriman, the spirit of darkness and evil, also contested for each human soul. Still, at the last judgment, "good" will win out, and man will reach immortal paradise, a pleasure garden. The dualism that arose from the idea of the dueling forces of "good" and "evil" has persisted to our time.

The Magi, who became superfluous under Cyrus and Zoroaster, were reinstated when Darius usurped the throne because the Magi helped his coup. Darius also married Cyrus's daughter to guarantee the coup of 521 BC. The Magi recorded Zoroaster's oral message in the Zend Avesta. They kept the duties of tending sacred fires (symbol of Ahura Mazda) and making astrological predictions for themselves. Their stargazing led them to Bethlehem centuries later.

Thus God prepared the world during the 800–200 BC time period. Religion was in the air. It was the spirit of the times! The Zeitgeist!

---

8. Ionians were at that time leaders of the Hellenic world culture. "Uvo Holscher has well put the case of the Phoenician and Egyptian origin of Ionic science and metaphysics" (William F. Albright).

Return to Judah

Many people wanted new insight into religion. The returning Jews were to tell these people about their God, who was sovereign over all creation and all history. Some Jews did want to reach out, as the book of Jonah showed was God's intent. Jonah was told to save Nineveh, but he shipped out to Tarshish instead. Storms buffeted the boat. Jonah told the sailors he was the cause, and they must toss him overboard. They did. With the help of a fish, he was deposited on the road to Nineveh. Jonah preached and saved the people, but he pouted when God let the people of Nineveh repent. Evidently, most of the Hebrews felt as he did, for in the end, they kept God for themselves—the chosen people.

The Hebrews became Jews in Babylon, a people who could exist through their religion without a country. Communities of Jews remained or formed in Babylon, Persia, Egypt, in Tarsus of Anatolia, and other places. These communities later provided a place for the first Christians to go when spreading the gospel. Perhaps that was God's intent all along.

In the meantime, the Jews who returned to Judah rebuilt the temple and Judaism with more rituals, laws, and legalisms than ever. They missed the whole point of the prophets—that they were to live righteously with law writ upon their hearts by the Holy Spirit rather than on voluminous scrolls. They extended to four scrolls the number 4 commandment of about four words: "Remember the Sabbath, keep it Holy."

Ezra, Nehemiah, Esther, Job, Jonah, Haggai, Zechariah, Malachi, and Chronicles were added to the Old Testament as Judah and the temple were rebuilt. There were no more prophets after 400 BC, although Daniel was probably written then.

During captivity in Babylon, Daniel was part of a group who received special instruction for a revival of Babylonian civilization. While Nebuchadnezzar appreciated reviving the past, he also built for the future. His walls, gates, buildings, monuments, canals, and hanging gardens were spectacular. Then he had a dream. Not only were his wise men to interpret the dream, but they were to tell him what the dream was. Daniel, too. So he prayed. And prayed. And he was answered.

Daniel told Nebuchadnezzar his dream.

> You looked and before you stood a large statue with a head of pure gold, chest and arms of silver, belly and thighs of bronze, legs of iron, feet of iron and baked clay. A rock came and struck the feet. Then the rest of the statue broke into pieces like chaff on a threshing floor. A wind swept the pieces away. The rock that struck the statue became a huge mountain and filled the whole earth. (Dan. 2:3 1–35, NIV)

Daniel interpreted the dream, but without the names we now assign to the kingdoms.

> You are the head of gold [Chaldean Babylon]. After you, another kingdom will rise, inferior to yours [Persia]. Next, a third kingdom, one of bronze, will rule over the whole earth [Hellenic Greeks] Finally there will be a fourth kingdom, strong as iron, for iron breaks and smashes everything, but it has feet partly of clay. It is a divided kingdom. [Roman was divided before it fell.] (Excerpts from Daniel 2:38–42, NIV)

> In the time of those kings, the God of heaven will set up a kingdom that will never be destroyed. This is the meaning of the rock cut out of the mountain but not by human hands—a rock that broke the iron, bronze, clay, silver and gold to pieces. The great God has shown the king what will take place in the future. (Dan. 2:44–45, NIV)

God, through Daniel, predicted the fall of four earthly empires broken by the rock cut from the mountain, but not by human hands. During this sequence of kingdoms, God will set up His kingdom through His Son, the rock. The kingdom of God will never be destroyed, for the mountain of the Lord will fill the world.

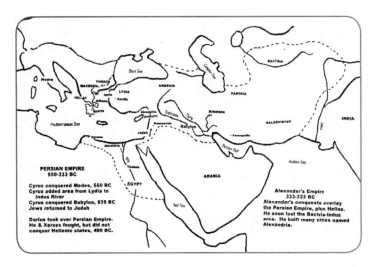

Remember that rising spiral of civilization mentioned earlier in this section? As the spiral rises in cultural development, it also spreads over more territory. These four civilizations of Daniel are to be added to the first two, Sumerian and Egyptian, with which the Hebrews came in contact in the Old Testament. This makes six and will be important later on—in the revelation to John.

The book of Daniel closed the Old Testament. William Foxwell Albright noted that the Old Testament was written using *empirical logic*, which rested on actual experience. He said the Old Testament has no trace of the abstract. The Old Testament was closed before Thales's formal logic filtered down from Ionia.

Another reason prophecy ceased was to protect it from too much Persian influence. Satan, as a tester and accuser then a tempter, probably came into the Bible from Persia, for he is not there before Job. The church has combated dualism ever since. If God had not shut the Old Testament, it may have sounded more like the Apocrypha. God probably wanted to limit this Persian influence.

The Persians were still influential. Their empire extended from Egypt to the Indus River and lasted two hundred years, thanks to the provincial system adopted from Assyria that allowed for self-rule in the provinces. From Assyria, Persia also adopted Babylonian science. The Aramaic language and alphabet inspired Persian as cuneiform died out.

Historians caution us not to overestimate Persian civilization. This is rather difficult to do with our overemphasis on the Greco-Roman base to Western civ. Ironically, Persians helped preserve Greek thought so it could return to the west. Persia influenced two brilliant periods of the future: Gupta India and Islamic civilization.

In the meantime, God used Persia to further his purpose. He anointed Cyrus to restore Judah in 530 BC. But He evidently had a mission for the Hellenic civilization, for Persia never conquered the Hellenic city-states.

Darius (who usurped Cyrus) and his son Xerxes tried by land and sea to conquer Hellas, ca. 480 BC. Their attempts produced heroic stories about Spartans who defended the pass at Thermopylae and about a marathon runner who ran twenty-six miles to inform Athens of a Hellenic victory over the Persians. Athens, Sparta, and other cities formed a league to fight Persia. Then formed leagues to fight one another. Although they formed many leagues, they never really learned how to govern beyond the city-state level, for which they wrote many constitutions.

During the Persian wars, Athens was destroyed but rebuilt to greater glory with much chiseling of marble and much crafting of words. Words! Words! Words! From Socrates who questioned everything until he drank the hemlock cocktail for abandoning old gods, through Plato who helped substitute philosophy for religion, to Aristotle who classified everything and tutored Alexander in Macedonia.

Alexander was primed to carry out his father's plan of empire. When Philip was murdered, Alexander announced, "Nothing has changed, except the name of the king." Alexander proceeded with his whirlwind conquest of the Medi-East: Anatolia in 334 BC, Syria in 333 BC, Tyre in 332 BC, Egypt in 331 BC, Persia in 330 BC. Another year, another conquest.

Alexander made a trip to the Indus to scout his Persian domains. On the way back, he collected specimens for Aristotle, but he immediately lost the remote eastern area. To secure the Persian west, he established Greek cities (seventeen were named Alexandria). He also married a Persian princess, but he died in 323 BC before his son was born to Roxanne.

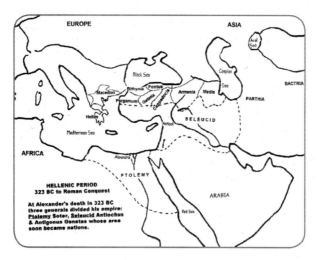

The empire was divided between his generals: Ptolemy in Egypt and Seleucid Antiochus in Persia. Both the Ptolemies and Seleucids endured because they rested on the strong foundation of old civilizations with people long accustomed to empire rule.

Macedon, Hellas, and northern Anatolia went to a third general but immediately broke into small nations. The idea of empire was beyond the grasp of their city-state mentality.

Still, it is amazing that the influence of Alexander's ten-year whirlwind conquest should last for nearly two centuries, 330–150 BC, while Hellenism spread around the east Mediterranean. The Old Testament was even translated into Greek by seventy Hebrew scholars imported to Egypt for the task. They produced the *Sept*uagint version (*sept* for seventy).

Perhaps God wanted Hellenic philosophy and formal logic to take the edge off religion and thus provide a climate that was more or less neutral to religion when Christ came into the world. When the Word became flesh and dwelt among us!

3

The Word Became Flesh

Medi-East Cycles of Civilization

At the Medi-East crossroads to three continents, the cycles of civilization turned more rapidly than elsewhere. The interchange of ideas produced a rising and expanding spiral of social evolution. God led the ragtag Hebrews into contact with five dominant civilizations in this rising spiral as their faith slowly evolved. In quick review, the five were the following:

Sumerian Civ

Abraham reached back to this earliest civilization for stories such as the flood, to which the Hebrews gave a religious interpretation. They recognized *one* God sovereign in all creation rather than pantheons of nature gods. God Almighty, El Shaddai, led Abraham to monotheism as God also led him from Ur to Haran and Canaan when the dynamic center of civilization shifted from the Persian Gulf to the Mediterranean.

Egyptic Civ

Abraham's descendants went to Egypt where they were enslaved for centuries yet grew from one tribe to twelve. God appeared to Moses as I Am, lord. He called Moses to lead the Hebrews back to Canaan.

God now began to reveal His providence in history. He reminded Israel over and over that He brought them out of Egypt. When they recited the events of the Exodus over and over, plus all the begats, the Hebrews developed a unique sense of time and history that was ongoing and purposeful as it reached back to the dawn of history, even to man's common origin.

It was no accident that God led the Hebrews back to Canaan when He did during the interim between superpowers—the only time small nations could exist. Israel had two centuries under their judges, 1220–1020 BC, and one century under kings Saul, David, and Solomon, 1020–922 BC. After Solomon died, the nation divided for two centuries, 922–722 BC. Israel, the ten tribes of the north, then fell to the Assyrians who, in turn, fell to the Chaldeans, 606 BC.

Babylonian Civ

The Chaldeans remained in Babylon atop Babylonian civilization, which was a conglomerate that began long before Hammurabi, ca. 1750 BC, and included Assyria's preservation of Babylonian culture, ca. 700 BC (this is why we still have a twenty-four-hour day). The Chaldeans took the remaining two tribes of the south, Judah and Benjamin, into captivity. In Babylon, the Hebrews learned that God was not restricted to the temple or to Jerusalem or even to Judah—all of which fell. God is universal. He is sovereign in all of creation and all of history.

Persian Civ

God anointed the king of an even more foreign nation, Cyrus of Persia, to release the captives from Babylon and to restore them in Judah. Returning Jews were to tell all nations about their universal God and to bring all nations to His holy mountain as the prophets had foretold.

While the prophets were telling Israel that all nations would come to their high holy mountain, God was preparing the world for their message. Universal religion was in the air between 800 and 200 BC. Pantheons of gods were crumbling all over the civilized world—in China, India, Persia, and Greece. But Judah failed to tell others about their God, who "anointed" Cyrus of Persia and used this foreign king to release them from captivity in Babylon.

Persia helped restore Judah and the temple. Restoration was Persia's policy in all its provinces. This initial gesture of goodwill was followed by a reasonable amount of self-rule in its provinces that stretched from Egypt to India. Although Persia tried to make a province of Hellas during the Persian Wars, 480 BC, the Hellenic city-states remained undefeated.

Hellenic Civ

Alexander conquered the Persian Empire, ca. 330 BC. Was this so that Hellenistic thought, especially formal logic and philosophy more or less untainted by religion, could be pasted onto civilization around the east Mediterranean? Hellenism succeeded all too well. The Jews in Alexandria even forgot their Hebrew so they had their scriptures translated into Greek in 168 BC. Seventy scholars were imported from Judah to assist in the translation. Thus, the name *Septuagint* was given to the Greek translation. The Hellenes were called Greeks by the Romans.

The Roman Empire

The Greeks could not imagine how the Romans emerged so quickly. Actually, they just failed to notice. About the same time that tribes of Indo-European Dorians migrated into Greece, Indo-Euro Latins settled among seven hills near the mouth of the Tiber River, ca. 1000 BC.

The Latins built a bridge over the Tiber, 750 BC, to collect tolls on trade between the Greek colonies in the south and the Etruscans in the north. The Etruscans soon took over Rome, which they rebuilt on a grid pattern using stone for roads, aqueducts, and baths. The similarity of the Etruscan style to that of Minoan Crete and Harappan India is probably due to a common ancestry in Anatolia.

The Latins ousted the tyrannical Etruscan kings and set up a republic with no kings but with two consuls, ca. 500 BC. They expanded into the rest of the Italian Peninsula then beyond the peninsula. This brought Rome into conflict with Greece and later Carthage. Romans absorbed Greek territory and culture. First they took the colonies in the boot of Italy then moved from the "heel" across the Adriatic to mainland Greece.

Conflict with Carthage resulted in three Punic Wars (*Punic* is derived from *Phoenician*). Romans won the first war after they captured a grounded Punic ship. They copied the ship plank for plank and built a hundred in two months! After Rome won the war, 264–241 BC, they took tribute and Sicily from Carthage then expanded into Sardinia and Corsica. Hannibal responded by marching his elephants from Africa through Spain over the Alps and into Italy. He plundered his way through Italy until he was defeated by Scipio, 202 BC. Rome took Spain and more tribute. After the third Punic War—no one ever crossed Rome a third time—Carthage was destroyed. Burned, plowed, and salted, according to legend. Who knows what was lost to history when their library was destroyed? North Africa became a Roman province.

About the same time that Carthage was destroyed, Corinth was also destroyed, ca. 150 BC. The two leading commercial centers on the Mediterranean! But instead of Rome taking the lead, Alexandria in Egypt and Antioch in Syria came to the fore. Rome preferred the economics of tolls, tribute, taxes, and later, tithes.

Rome also looked to Gaul (France) for spoils and riches such as furs and ores. The crafty Carthaginians attributed these to Gaul to keep their source secret, probably America, although this is debated. And the records were destroyed.

In pursuit of Gaul's riches, Julius Caesar led an eight-year campaign against the Celts in 60 BC. It began at La Tene, strategically located in the Swiss Alps near the sources of the Rhine–Rhone–Danube Rivers. The Helvetii Celts decided to leave La Tene so they burned all their forts, villages, and fields behind them. Caesar forced the Helvetii to return and caught them filing through a pass at Lake Geneva. By Caesar's account, two hundred thousand were slaughtered. The remaining one hundred thousand returned to their burned-out homeland.

Caesar also recorded the crucial sea battle off the coast of Brittany in 55 BC. Coastal Celts were skilled sailors whose chiefs united in a maritime alliance. The Celtic fleet had 220 ships: high-prowed, flat-keeled (for shallow estuaries), with tall masts and sails of beaten hides. (Leather was more serviceable in Atlantic storms than the Egyptian linen of the Romans.) The ships were propelled solely by wind, for no Celt would demean himself by rowing. They even sailed into the wind to Caesar's amazement. Celts rained spears and arrows onto the decks of the Romans, who tried to ram the Celtic ships protected by iron chains that bound them against the buckling action of ocean rollers. (Romans used ropes.)

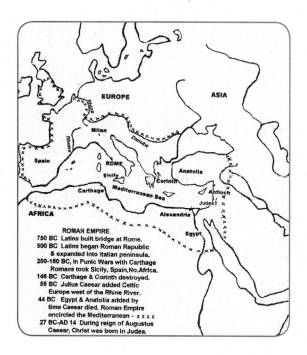

The Romans resorted to falces, sharp hooks thrown into the rigging, then pulled taut to cut the cordage. When the Celtic admiral saw the havoc, he tried to withdraw, but the wind suddenly stilled. Celts were becalmed. Roman galleys rowed over. Grappling irons were thrown, and the ships pulled together. Romans boarded for hand-to-hand combat. The entire Celtic fleet was destroyed or captured while Romans had eighty ships left. With these, Caesar later invaded Britain.

The battle ended Celtic seafaring, except for Ireland and also Scandinavia where the Vikings emerged. The crucial battle also ended connections with America, although civilization was already taken to America by seafarers in BC centuries.

Was the calming of the wind and the defeat of the Celts, plus the earlier defeat of Carthage, an accident? Or the providence of God? These defeats finally wiped out Baal worship—the bane of the Hebrews since time immemorial. Virtually nothing was left in its place, except emperor worship, a wide assortment of cults, and the dying remains of pantheons of gods.

Was God preparing the region for Christianity? First, by eradicating Baal. Then by extending the Roman Empire into Europe and around the entire Mediterranean.

After Caesar defeated the Celts, he persuaded the Ptolemies in Egypt, namely Cleopatra, to accept Roman rule. He followed this conquest with his trip to Anatolia in 47 BC. Caesar boasted, "I came, I saw, I conquered," even though Pompey had already secured the east Mediterranean for the Roman Empire. Either Pompey or Caesar granted Roman citizenship to the people of Tarsus, including Paul's father. This assured that Paul would be a Roman citizen.

Caesar returned in triumph to Rome, still a republic but on the road to decay. Cicero (106–43 BC) exhorted for a return to the stoic values of the early republic and for human rights, which included duty, decency, and honor—even among his fellow senators. He coined a new word, *humanitas*, but to no avail. In 44 BC, Caesar was named dictator for life.

By the Ides of March, Caesar's life was over. Caesar's will, which was out of date, named his nephew Octavian as his successor. Octavian had to fight for his inheritance. He finally defeated Marc Antony and Cleopatra at Actium on the west coast of Greece in 31 BC. Marc and Cleo returned to Egypt and committed suicide. Octavian returned to Rome and became the first emperor, Caesar Augustus. He ruled until AD 14. The Roman Empire was at its imperial peak.

A Census Statistic in Imperial Rome

Jesus was born in the backwater province of Judea during the reign of Augustus. He was no more than an insignificant census statistic hardly worth noting compared to the grandeur of the Augustan age of imperial Rome. Yet in three hundred years, Christianity would become the state religion of a divided Roman Empire. In four hundred years, while the Roman West lay crumbling, Christianity would lay the foundation for a new Western civilization.

Was this an accident? Or the providence of God!

Imperial Rome kept a tight rein on its provinces. They allowed no hint of insurrection. In Judea, Herod caused much turmoil over the birth of Jesus. He even slaughtered infants of his own people. Zealots preached revolt. Others in the hierarchy collaborated with Rome. Jesus preached the strangest message of all. He overturned Judaic law, or so his people thought, yet he instructed them to render unto Caesar the taxes and political rule that belonged to Rome. God was using Rome to further His purpose, for God *is* sovereign over all nations and all history. Besides, God's kingdom is of the spirit.

Jesus was the person, the individual, who took mankind into the realm of the spirit. He was the Word become flesh. He was the Lord Jesus, a divine human being. Luke introduced this idea beautifully in the story of Mary visited by the Holy Spirit. When Jesus was baptized by John the Baptist, God acknowledged His kinship with the words, "This is my beloved Son."

Through Christ, God made a spiritual covenant sealed with a dove, the symbol of the Holy Spirit. All the separations of mankind—from God, from creation, and from society—would now be reconciled. What God *purposed* in Christ was

> to be put into effect when the times will have reached their fulfillment…to bring all things in heaven and on earth together under one head, even Christ. (Eph. 1:10, NIV)

The Lord Jesus was and *is* the unity of all things in heaven and earth, all of the spiritual, and all of the physical.

Jesus's ministry showed the way. He was the way to *know* God, to have unity and intimacy with God. In order to accomplish this, Jesus tried to raise people above man-made laws, even above the i-dotting religious laws of Judaism, to spiritual *one*ness with

God. Mankind was freed from the law of society and religion but was bound by the law of the spirit—law writ upon the heart—which was even more binding. It was not only physical acts but the very *ideas* held and cherished in the heart, mind, and soul of each person that mattered.

This may be seen in the way Jesus reduced the Ten Commandments to two, which go back to the Old Testament. Jesus explained,

> The first is "Hear, O Israel: The LORD our God, the LORD is one; and you shall love the LORD your God with all your heart, with all your soul, with all your mind and with all your strength [Deut. 6:4-5 NIV]." The second is this, "You shall love your neighbor as yourself [Lev. 19:18, RSV]." (Mark 12:29–31)

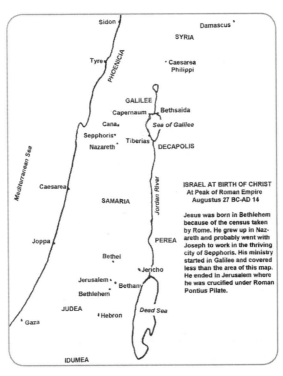

ISRAEL AT BIRTH OF CHRIST
At Peak of Roman Empire
Augustus 27 BC-AD 14

Jesus was born in Bethlehem because of the census taken by Rome. He grew up in Nazareth and probably went with Joseph to work in the thriving city of Sepphoris. His ministry started in Galilee and covered less than the area of this map. He ended in Jerusalem where he was crucified under Roman Pontius Pilate.

The imperative is to love God, not mankind or humanity, but *God*. When we put God first, this raises and relates us to the only absolute—to God. More than that, we are to love God with all our heart and strength (our physical being), also with all our mind, and with all our soul. This relates a balanced whole three-dimensional human being, not someone stagnated at a physical, emotional level or someone off on a spiritualistic tangent. When we also love God with our minds, we have a balanced, intelligent whole religion. If not, the result is what we have today: too much soap-opera emotionalism or too much surrealistic spiritualism, not enough intelligent understanding of God's Word.

God gave us a mind to use. God breathed spirit and thought into man so we may truly *know* Him. It was in the mind of man, with Adam and Eve, that separation occurred; for God Is, whether we acknowledge Him or not. So it is in the mind that man will be reconciled, that he will ultimately and intimately know God.

We cannot know without a foundation of basic instruction. Jesus received his in the synagogue at Nazareth. Synagogues, which originated in Babylon, were the educational centers of each village. Ten married men could organize one, mainly to instruct their sons. Jesus certainly spent more time in the synagogue at Nazareth than in the temple at Jerusalem. At twelve, he went to Jerusalem for Passover and went to the temple "to be about his Father's business."

Twenty years later, Jesus again celebrated Passover in Jerusalem at his Last Supper with his disciples in the upper room. On Maundy Thursday afternoon, the lambs of Passover were slain by worshippers in the temple, 250,000 lambs according to Josephus. William Barclay explained,

> Between the worshipper and altar [at the curtain that separated the Holy of Holies] were two long lines of priests, each with a bowl. As the lamb's throat was slit by the worshipper, the blood was caught in a bowl and passed

up the line, until the priest at the end of the line dashed it upon the altar, as Moses had done at Sinai.[1]

The entrails and fat were extracted for the sacrifice, and the carcass was handed back to the worshipper for the Passover meal at sundown with family or friends, about ten people. The Passover meal consisted of the lamb roasted on a spit, unleavened bread, bitter herbs, fruit paste, and wine. All had a special meaning that went back to the Passover at the Exodus. As they were eating in the upper room,

> Jesus took bread, gave thanks and broke it, and gave it to his disciples, "Take, eat…this is my body." He took the cup, gave thanks…and said, "This is my blood of the covenant which is being poured out for many." (Mark 14:22, NIV)

Jesus was the lamb. He was the sacrifice. Sufficient for all time, for all people! No other sacrifice—animal or human—need ever be made again. Just think what this has meant in the world. We take it for granted now, but only five hundred years ago, the Aztecs were sacrificing humans by cutting out their beating hearts.

After his last supper, Jesus went to the Garden of Gethsemane to pray:

> Abba, Father, everything is possible for you. Take this cup from me. Yet not what I will, but what you will. (Mark 14:36, NIV)

When Jesus rose from prayer, Judas arrived with the crowds. Jesus was betrayed by his own disciple and convicted by his own

---

1. William Barclay, *The Gospel of Mark* (Philadelphia: Westminster Press, 2001), 332–333. By Josephesus's count, over two million were in Jerusalem for Maundy Thursday. Another source says the population of Jerusalem was 50,000, with 250,000 for Maundy Thursday.

people in a mock trial. Mark recorded the last words Jesus spoke at his trial. The high priest asked,

> "Are you the Christ, the Son of the Blessed?" Jesus said, "I am; and you will see the Son of Man sitting at the right hand of Power, and coming with the clouds of heaven." (Mark 14:61–62, RSV)

The high priest tore his clothes and cried, "Blasphemy!" The crowds agreed. Jesus deserved to die. Peter denied Jesus three times. The cock crowed. Judas hung himself. The trial went to Pontius Pilate for sentencing. Pilate washed his hands of the matter after the people clamored for the crucifixion of Jesus and the release of Barabbas.

When Jesus died on the cross, "the curtain in the temple was torn in two from top to bottom" (Mark 15:38, NIV). A veil no longer separated people from God. Jesus reconciled us with God. He died to "atone" for our sin so we may be "at one" with God. Separate yet one with the Father as the Lord Jesus was. Lord means the Son of God. Jesus means the Son of Man. Jesus acknowledged he was the Son of God, but just as often, he referred to himself as the Son of Man, as he did in his last words at his trial: "From now on, the Son of Man will be seated at the right hand of God." But no one understood.

Pentecost and Persecution

After Jesus's resurrection from the tomb and before his ascension, he commissioned his disciples:

> Go...baptize in the name of the Father, Son and Holy Spirit, and teach what I have commanded you. And lo, I am with you always, to the close of the age. (Matt. 28:19–20, RSV)

THE RIGHT HAND OF GOD

Just before his ascension, Jesus gave the disciples his last instructions. They were to wait in Jerusalem a few days for the Holy Spirit. At Pentecost, the Holy Spirit, the cloud of heaven, filled the people. They felt a wind, saw tongues of fire, and *all* were able to understand Peter's message in his own language.

> God has raised this Jesus to life, and we are all witnesses. Exalted to the right hand of God, he has received from the Father the promised Holy Spirit and has poured out what you now see and hear. God has made this Jesus, whom you crucified both Lord and Christ. (Acts 2:32, 36, NIV)

Three thousand were added that day. Those who had stayed in Jerusalem after Passover now took Peter's message home with them. Pentecost was the birth of the church.

Persecution at the hands of Orthodox Judaism forced the disciples into the world. Again, God's providence in disguise. The persecutions caused a rift in Judeo-Christian relations. The rift is best seen in the life of Saul, who became Paul. Saul was born a Roman citizen in Tarsus, the capital and trade center of Cilicia in Anatolia. He was exposed to Greek culture, including formal logic, before he went to Jerusalem to further his position in Judaism. Staunchly orthodox, Saul sanctioned the persecution of the new heresy, which spread in spite of what they did.

So many new converts were made that the disciples decided they needed "deacons" to tend to daily affairs and care of widows and the poor. Stephen, a man full of faith and the Holy Spirit, was chosen with six other men. Stephen did great wonders. Opposition rose against him. Leaders persuaded "stooges" to say they heard Stephen speak words of blasphemy against God.

In chapter 7 of Acts, Stephen defended himself before the Sanhedrin. He said, "Brothers and fathers, listen to me" (Acts 7:2, NIV). He recited the entire history of the Jews as he pointed out how stiff-necked they were. They always resisted the Holy

Spirit. They never listened to God or the prophets. And now they betrayed and murdered the Righteous One. The Sanhedrin was furious.

But Stephen, full of the Holy Spirit, looked up to heaven and saw the glory of God and Jesus standing at the right hand of God. Stephen exclaimed, "Look, I see heaven open and the Son of Man standing at the right hand of God" (Acts 7:55, NIV).[2]

Stephen ended his trial with the very same words that Jesus had ended his. Stephen saw what Jesus foresaw, for now it was accomplished.

The Son of man, the Son of mankind since man's common origin in Genesis throughout all of history, is now standing at the forefront of future history. At God's "right hand," Jesus will lead God's providence in history. These two simple phrases encompass all of BC and AD history.

Thanks to Owen Barfield, this may now be understood. Barfield pointed out that

> because Christ, the Second Person of the Trinity, is recognized as a historical event in time, therefore…between the First and Third Persons, all history, in a manner, lies.[3]

This is why the Hebrews were given their unique sense of history so we may grasp a Lord Jesus concept that comprehends the Christ event within the entire sweep of history. All of BC history is contained in the phrase *Son of Man*, and all of AD history in the phrase *at the Right Hand of God*. This includes what is yet to come, for Christ is at the forefront leading the way.

The many believers who returned home after Pentecost spread the news about Jesus's resurrection and about Pentecost. Philip helped an Ethiopian who was reading Isaiah while riding home

---

2. *Heaven open* means the "spiritual revealed."
3. Barfield, *Saving the Appearances*, 165.

in his chariot. Philip explained that the words of Isaiah were fulfilled in Jesus.

Peter was called to Caesarea by Cornelius, a Roman centurion, whose family were God-fearers. Peter had a vision of a sheet that contained all kinds of animals, reptiles, and birds. A voice said, "Get up, Peter. Kill and eat. Nothing God has made is unclean." Peter saw that God was sending him to a Gentile. When he spoke to Cornelius's household, the Holy Spirit came upon all of them. The Holy Spirit led the way, so an amazed Peter followed by baptizing the Gentiles.

Saul persecuted "people of the way" in Jerusalem. He left for Damascus to continue persecutions. On the road to Damascus, Saul was blinded by a light and the words of Jesus, "Saul, why do you persecute me?" God sent Ananias to bring Saul to the city. Saul's sight was restored, and he was converted. Saul preached. Jews tried to kill him. For protection, Saul was sent to Tarsus.

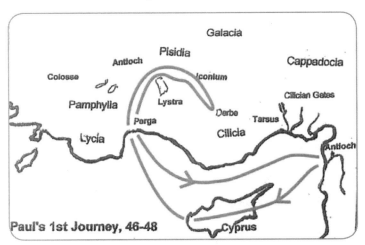

Paul's 1st Journey, 46–48

Tarsus was Saul's home, where he had been exposed to Greek culture. So when the Jews rejected Saul, he knew the Lord "made him a light for Gentiles" (Acts 13:47, NIV). After a while, Barnabas brought Saul back to Antioch. People were first called Christians at Antioch.

Saul went with Barnabas on his first missionary journey (AD 46–48). While on Cyprus, Saul changed his name to Paul. When they left Cyprus to go to Perga, Mark gave up and went back home, so Paul did not want Mark on their second trip. Barnabas stood by Mark.

Paul teamed up with Silas for his second journey through Syria and Cilicia. At Lystra, they met Timothy, who joined them. As Paul went beyond his first journey, they came to the Sea of Marmara (between the Mediterranean and Black Seas). Paul intended to go east to Asia, but he was stopped, so he went to Troas. That night he had a dream. A man called him to Macedonia in Europe instead of Asia. (Luke now shifts to *we* in recording Acts, because this is when Luke joined Paul.) In Macedonia, they went to Philippi, Thessalonica, Corinth, and back to Anatolia to found a church at Ephesus. Paul's third journey was to revisit the churches he started, so it was much like the second, except he began at Ephesus.

The turn to Europe was a crucial turning point in Christianity. By God's providence, with Jesus at His right hand leading it, apostles remained in Roman territory. Was God protecting Christianity from more sophisticated civilizations in the East so they could start a new Western civilization in Europe on a solid Christian foundation?

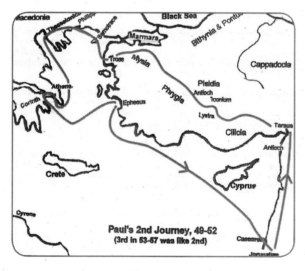

Paul's 2nd Journey, 49-52
(3rd in 53-57 was like 2nd)

Apostles suffered persecution at the hands of the Romans as Jesus said they would. They awaited his second coming. When they realized the second coming was not to be in their lifetimes but in God's time, Mark, Matthew, Luke, and John wrote their Gospels. Luke added the Acts of the Holy Spirit, for the Holy Spirit led the apostles in establishing the early church. Paul wrote letters to the churches he established, including one to Rome where he was later placed under house arrest. Peter was already in Rome, where he established the church. Thus, he was the first pope (perhaps retroactively but well-deserved). Peter was executed by Nero in a wholesale lot of Christians after the fire in AD 64. Paul too, perhaps.

These poor persecuted Christians and those fed to the lions may have doubted the providential blessing of Christianity's move to Rome and to Europe. The bleak times became even bleaker when the temple in Jerusalem was destroyed in 70. After another insurrection in 135, the Jews were dispersed, and Judea was renamed Palestine. Romans were always quite thorough when provoked a third time.

Revelation—Then and Now

Amid the persecutions, the Christians had the Revelation to John for comfort. The Revelation assured them of the absolute sovereignty of God and the ultimate destruction of evil *after* much tribulation. In the meantime, there was spiritual inner peace for those who were faithful to God and the Lamb. In the end, there was the promise of fulfillment with the Second Coming of the Lord Jesus Christ and the "new" Jerusalem, when all people will know God. Man's common destiny, ever since his common origin in the Garden of Eden, *will* be fulfilled.

Revelation was written to seven of the churches in Anatolia, which Paul established at Ephesus, Smyrna, Pergamum, Thyatira,

Sardis, Philadelphia, and Laodicea. The message to them covered the here-and-now part of Revelation.

John was then shown what "was to come." A time of tribulation in three sets of woes, represented by seven seals, seven trumpets, and seven bowls. Six of each set unleashed terrible woes upon the people. The seventh of each set was a reprieve or led to a reprieve. Finally, a voice with the seventh trumpet announced,

> The kingdom of the world has become the Kingdom of our Lord and His Christ and He will reign forever and ever. (Rev. 11:15, NIV)

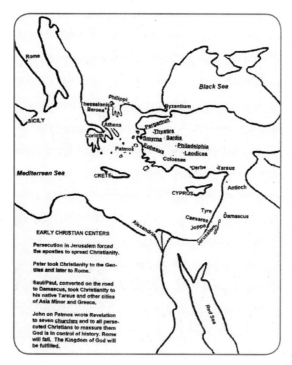

EARLY CHRISTIAN CENTERS

Persecution in Jerusalem forced the apostles to spread Christianity.

Peter took Christianity to the Gentiles and later to Rome.

Saul/Paul, converted on the road to Damascus, took Christianity to his native Tarsus and other cities of Asia Minor and Greece.

John on Patmos wrote Revelation to seven churches and to all persecuted Christians to reassure them God is in control of history. Rome will fall. The Kingdom of God will be fulfilled.

Eventually, yes, but not for a while. Revelation was a controversial book. It was the last to be included in the canon. Martin Luther wanted to delete it. The message, as interpreted in the first century and in the 1500s, was different from the message that the latter-born, with two thousand years of hindsight plus insight, are able to understand. We do not have to go through all the surrealistic interpretations of the past as we look for a simpler present-day meaning.

Abraham's sacrifice of Isaac was more understandable with Kierkegaard's explanation from his nineteenth-century perspective. Revelation also takes on new meaning from a twentieth-century perspective.

Revelation 12 is about the woman and the dragon. The woman is the Judeo-Christian religion, and the dragon is everything arraigned against her. The woman, as Judaism, has twelve stars in her crown. She gave birth to a son, Jesus. When the dragon tried to devour him—crucify him—the son was taken up to God and His throne, where Christ now sits at His right hand.

The woman as Christianity then fled to a desert, a place of refuge. The Roman conquest of Western Europe prepared a place of refuge for Christianity. Paul was called to Europe to take Christianity to this refuge. In Western Europe, a few centuries after Paul, Christianity laid the foundation of Western civilization through the Roman Catholic Church.

The dragon still pursued the woman.

> She was given the two wings of a great eagle so that she might fly to the place prepared for her in the desert, where she would be taken care of for a time, times and a half time, safe from the serpent's reach. (Rev. 12:13–14, NIV)

Christianity, with the wings of an eagle, flew from Europe to America, which is represented by the eagle. There it was safe and renewed for three and a half times. The time units may be days or, more likely, centuries. Thus, during seventeenth, eighteenth, nineteenth, and half of the twentieth century, Christianity was safe and thrived in America. The people's closeness to God the Creator and His creation was renewed on each new frontier.

This is another miraculous turning point of the Paul-to-Europe sort. America was discovered just in time to provide a refuge for Protestants so they could found a new nation based on the reformed Judeo-Christian tradition. Was this an accident? Or was it God's providence with Jesus leading that providence?

Revelation 17 also has a passage that we can interpret more accurately from our twentieth-century vantage point. The passage is about a woman on a beast in a sea of chaos. This woman is *not* the Judeo-Christian faith as in Revelation 12. She now represents civilization. She is a prostitute who caused kings and leaders to misuse—to prostitute—the culture and civilization entrusted to them. The seven-headed beast she rides represents knowledge. Man's accumulated fund.

> The woman was arrayed in purple and scarlet...on her forehead was written a name of mystery. "Babylon the great, mother of harlots and of the earth's abominations" And I saw the woman drunk with the blood of saints and...martyrs of Jesus. When I saw her I marveled greatly. But the angel said to me, "Why marvel? I will tell you the mystery of the woman, and the beast with seven heads and ten horns that carries her...This calls for a mind with wisdom. The seven heads are seven hills on which the woman is seated; they are also seven kings, five of whom have fallen, one is, the other has not yet come and when he comes he must remain only a little while." (Rev. 17:4–7; 9–10, RSV)

The woman is civilization. Babylon represented the worst evils of civilization to the Jews. (Besides, John had to be cryptic. He could not say she had Rome stamped on her forehead.) The beast is knowledge. In Genesis, the words *Eve, serpent, reveal,* and *beast* are similar. The serpent represented wisdom or knowledge, which the beast also symbolized. Now applied to Roman civ, the woman is seated on the beast with seven heads, which are the seven hills of Rome.

The seven heads are also seven kings or seven civilizations that accumulated mankind's fund of knowledge. The harlot riding the beast of knowledge means she has prostituted, misused, mankind's fund of knowledge. So the beast is in a sea of chaos. Knowledge is in chaos at the end of the twentieth century.

The five kings, or civilizations, already fallen were those the Hebrews came in contact with in BC centuries: 1) Sumerian, 2) Egyptian, 3) Babylonian, 4) Persian, and 5) Hellenic. The one that *is*, and was implied to fall, was *Roman*. The other "yet to come" and "to remain only a while" must be Western civilization.

Of course, there were other civilizations, but these are the ones in a direct line of ascent that Judeo-Christians came in close contact with. The Jews wandered through the first five when each was dominant in the area. Christianity became the driving force in the last two. The area of each succeeding civilization increased in size until today, when Western civ is on all continents—at least, its technology is.

Please see the spiral civilization chart and color-coded map at the front of the book near the contents.

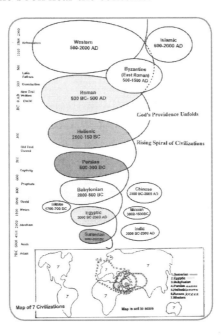

The Revelation to John at the end of the first century completed the writing of the New Testament. William F. Albright pointed out that its timing was as providential as that of the Old Testament, which used only empirical logic (from actual experience) with no trace of formal logic. Paul, however, made "full use of formal logic in his close reasoning in the NT."

Also, the New Testament was written when Christian thought was balanced between Essene and Gnostic extremes. Thus a balanced human-divine understanding of Jesus was put into the New Testament, even though the church has swung from overemphasizing the humanity to overemphasizing the divinity of Christ ever since. Essenes emphasized the humanity of Christ and looked for an earthly Messiah and earthly solutions yet withdrew into monasteries and removed themselves from contact with the world. On the other hand, Gnostics emphasized spirit (pneuma) and denied humanity. Yet many partook of earthly living as if the body were completely separate from and unrelated to the spirit. At a time between these extremes, a balanced divine-human Lord Jesus was put into the New Testament.

New Testament canon was established ca. 200 after much sifting and sorting of manuscripts, plus much discussion in the strong Christian centers that existed in Alexandria, Antioch, Ephesus, Corinth, Rome, and Carthage. The church spread throughout North Africa, Anatolia, Greece, and Italy, also into Spain and France.

Christianity Rose as Rome Fell

As Christianity grew and spread, the Roman Empire declined. After a series of disastrous Nero-type emperors, the situation improved with four emperors from the provinces: Trajan from Spain, Hadrian the builder (Hadrian's Wall in England), Antonius the pious, and Marcus Aurelius the philosopher-king. The four ruled from 98 to 180.

THE RIGHT HAND OF GOD

About 150 human rights that went beyond citizen's rights were recognized by law. This was the Roman contribution to mankind: human rights beyond the constitutional law of the Greeks or the statute law of Babylonians under Hammurabi. Cicero's *humanitas* finally prevailed as the Romans put humanity at the *center* of the universe. But in little more than a century, the human rights were gone—under military "barracks" emperors and the squeeze for taxes.

Since taxes were now equal all over the empire, they fell hardest on Rome and the Italian Peninsula, which had no economic base to produce the taxes. Food production was farmed out to the provinces. People moved from the country and contact with nature to urban living with few jobs except in government and public works, for there was little industry or commerce. But there was much consumption of goods from the Medi-East and India. Roman gold funneled through Egypt and out the Red Sea to fund Indic glory. India added "arabic" numbers, zero, quadratic equations, etc., to mankind's fund of knowledge. A thousand years later, the numbers came to Western civ through Islamic civ, so they were called *arabic* numbers and not *indic*.

Inevitably, political power gravitated toward economic and cultural soundness in the east Mediterranean. Around 300, Emperor Diocletion drew a fateful line just west of Greece, which divided the Roman east from the Roman west. He restructured government with two rulers in the east at Nicomedia and Sirmium and two in the west at Milan and Trier. The Caesars at Sirmium and Trier were to succeed their Augustuses at Nicomedia and Milan, who were to retire after a certain term of office. The two in the west just happened to retire and expire at the same time, so their sons fought to rule. There went peaceful succession.

Constantine of Trier saw a flaming cross in the sky and decided to fight with, rather than against, Christianity. He defeated Maxentius of Milan. In 313, Constantine issued the

Edict of Milan, which restored confiscated property and freedom of worship to Christians. When rulers in the east continued to persecute Christians, Constantine took over the whole empire.

In 326, Constantine built a new capital, Constantinople, dedicated to Christianity. Strategically located on the peninsula site of old Byzantium, it was easily defended with water on three sides and with an eleven-mile wall on the landside. Constantinople was also on the east-west trade route to China and India, so a 10 percent surcharge could be exacted on trade passing through to keep his coffers full. Plus, it was at the center of Christianity, which provided an underlying unity and a dynamic impetus to the emerging Christian empire.

Constantine made Christianity the state religion, so he felt that he controlled the church. He called the councils and issued edicts to strengthen Christianity. Now that persecution was more than a lion's gulp away, Christians had the luxury to debate theology. And debate they did—in the marketplace, at the barbershop. Was Christ fully God and/or fully man? What was his relation to God?

Alexandria in Egypt was the hub of debate in North Africa. Origen was an Alexandrian Greek, ca. 200, when the New Testament canon was being discussed and sorted out. He examined the nature of God, the divinity of Christ, also salvation and free will. He began systematic Christian theology. He also developed the allegorical method of interpreting the Bible rather than literal interpretation.

Arius from Libya said Christ was not fully God but was created by God as an intermediary-emissary. Arius gave his name to Arianism. Unfortunately, the Goths were converted to Arian Christianity before it was declared a heresy. This was while they were still living in their Indo-European homeland at the mouth of the Danube on the Black Sea.

Athanasius, bishop of Alexandria, opposed Arius and supported the fully God-fully man concept. People actually debated the issue in the marketplace and the barber chair. Constantine did not like all the debate. He wanted the issue settled, so he called the Council of Nicea in 325. The council adopted Athanasius's fully God-fully man doctrine and wrote the Nicene Creed to affirm it. By 381, all else was heresy, which made Gothic heretics fair game.

Church organization followed the government pattern with ecclesiastical sees, dioceses, etc. The political line that divided the east and west Roman Empire also divided the church into Eastern Orthodox and Roman Catholic. The two would evolve differently because the emperor in the East controlled the church while church power was divided between patriarchs at Alexandria, Antioch, Constantinople, and Jerusalem. The West had only one patriarch at Rome. He was able to concentrate power because he did not have to share it with other patriarchs. Also, Western emperors lost power, mostly by default, as they cowered in Ravenna while the Roman patriarch filled the void.

Latin Fathers

Around 400, three Latin fathers—Ambrose, Jerome, Augustine—each made contributions that firmly established the Roman church in the West. Gradually, the authority of the church prevailed over civil authority. Also, the sacrament of communion replaced baptism in importance. First-generation Christians, including Constantine, postponed baptism until they were near death in order to be certain their worst sins were behind them when they were cleansed by baptism. Second-generation Christians began to be baptized at birth, so communion was emphasized in the cleansing of sins. *Ex*communication then carried much clout for the church.

Latin Father Ambrose was influential in both these changes. Ambrose was born in Gaul (340), the son of a Roman prefect and educated in Rome for a career as a government official at Milan. During a conflict after the Bishop of Milan died, Ambrose gave such a persuasive address to settle a dispute between orthodox and Arian Christians that he was elected bishop. He put his family in the care of a brother and transferred his estates, his talents, and his training to the church. He preached moving sermons to combat a return to paganism. These converted Augustine.

The most dramatic incident for Ambrose was the penance he demanded of Theodosius. Theo had been emperor at Constantinople for ten years and felt imperial infallibility. He avenged the death of one soldier by slaughtering seven thousand people in an amphitheater. Ambrose refused to give Theo communion until public penance was made. Theo complied. Theo then issued an edict imposing Christianity as the state religion and outlawing all others under penalty of deportation.

In four hundred years, Christianity went from persecuted to protected to privileged!

Jerome, the second Latin father of the Roman church, was born in Yugoslavia of wealthy parents, ca. 340. He worried about the sudden wealth and privilege of the church, so he started a monastery in Bethlehem. (Monasticism rose to purify the church.) Jerome was always at the center of controversy, writing commentaries and firing off a few at the pope. The pope urged him to go to Bethlehem and translate the Bible into Latin Vulgate, the vernacular of the day. That should keep Jerome out of the pope's hair for a while. Jerome also advocated celibacy to purify the church, so he left Peter's mother-in-law out of his Latin Bible.

With the widespread use of Latin in the church, it became the legal and literary language of Europe. The common use of Jerome's Latin Vulgate helped bind together both the Roman church and the rising Western civilization as the political empire of Rome fell in the west.

Augustine, third Latin father (354–430), was born in Numidia, North Africa, perhaps of Punic ancestry. His father had a country estate at Tagaste. His mother, Monica, became a Christian as a young girl. His father converted in old age and died when Augustine was seventeen. Monica used resources her husband left her and went to Carthage with Augustine. He studied rhetoric and Latin. Carthage was a major city, but still in "provincial" North Africa. Augustine wanted to go to Rome. By then, he had a concubine, unnamed, and a son named Adeodatus. He took them and Monica with him to Rome.

In Carthage, Augustine had studied many philosophies. He became a Manichaeist, 378. Their philosophy suited his lifestyle, for they believed, "If the devil does counsel sin, then guilt does not ensue." Augustine's Manichaean friends helped him gain a position as a teacher of rhetoric in Milan. At age thirty, he and his family went to Milan. He soon sent away his concubine since he began to look for a "suitable" wife who could advance his position.

In Milan, Augustine was converted by Ambrose, who preached moving sermons against a return to paganism. Conversion caused Augustine enough anguish to prompt his *Confessions*, also his concept of original sin and predestination. Pelagius in Britain spoke out *for* free will and against predestination, which could become fatalism. Pelagius's ideas were declared heresy. (This needs some rethinking, for we *do* have free will.)

Augustine returned to Africa. Waiting for a boat at the port of Ostia, Monica died. Adeodatus died a few years later. Augustine and friends moved into his family property at Tagaste. There he wrote his *Confessions*. Once Augustine started confessing his sins and professing his faith, the church recognized his talent. He was drafted to become a priest during a visit to Hippo. When the bishop of Hippo died, he was appointed bishop. From there, he settled controversies in the church.

Donatists thought they were the only pure priests because they did not hand over books during persecutions. They felt that only when *they* administered the sacraments were the rites valid and effective. Augustine insisted the effect of a sacrament depended on the presence of Christ and attitude of recipient, not the purity of the minister. That settled the controversy.

Augustine also settled the Manichaeist controversy. Manichaeism was a cult derived from Zoroaster, but named for Mani. Since he once supported Manichaeism, Augustine was now able to refute the good-evil dualism of Manichaeism. Augustine declared that all is good in God's creation while evil is a lack of conformity to God's creative will rather than a force in itself.

But a new force was invading Europe, Mongol Huns from Asia. Indo-Euro tribes north of the Black Sea fled before them. Visigoths (West Goths) crossed the Danube into the Roman east. Theodosius sent them west. He half promised them land in the west, but the land was not forthcoming. After years of waiting, Alaric led his Visigoths in the sack of Rome in 410. Alaric died and was buried under a river. The Visigoths finally settled in Southern France and Spain.

When Rome was sacked, refugees fled to their estates in North Africa. They questioned whether the new Christian religion caused the sacking. It happened only two decades after Theodosius made it the state religion while Rome had been safe for centuries under the old gods. Augustine wrote *The City of God* to refute the idea. Even though the earthly city of Rome might fall, the spiritual city of God was eternal.

Thus, Augustine wrote the obituary that closed the Roman age as he opened the new age of Western civ with a new underlying "philosophy"—or rather, theology. He put God at the center of the universe instead of humanity, as Romans had the priority ever since Cicero's *humanitas.*

Vandals wrote the obituary for Augustine. They were the next wave of Goths to flee from the Huns. They swept through Roman territory to Spain, then into North Africa. In the process, they gave their name to *vandalism.* During their siege of Hippo in 430, Augustine died.

Fortunately, Augustine had already written the obituary to the fall of Rome in his *City of God.* As the Roman West was crumbling, a new Western civilization was beginning in Europe and France. Christianity was the dynamic force that would shape Western civilization, for God was at the center of their universe.

What a turn of events! From Augustus to Augustine! From the power of the Roman Empire to the power of the Roman Church! An accident? Or because an insignificant census statistic was now sitting at the right hand of God leading God's providence in history?

4

The Founding of
Western Civilization

Roman Church in Western Europe

The Roman Empire in the west declined rapidly after 400. The Roman East evolved into the Byzantine civilization and lasted for another one thousand years.

Inept rulers in the west failed to cope with Celts and Goths who sought refuge from the Mongol Huns. A strong emperor could have made a federation of all the new *foederati* kingdoms. Instead, the emperors cowered in Ravenna while some of the best-trained Roman administrators served the church, such as Ambrose of Milan who converted Augustine.

Augustine's *City of God* and his other writings put God at the center of the universe to provide the underlying dynamic of the new society. This, along with the unity provided by the Latin Bible of Jerome and with the strong church administration provided by

Ambrose, enabled Pope Gregory I—the fourth Latin father ca. 600—to strengthen the Roman church in Europe as it laid the foundation of Western civilization.

Europe was completely changed by the Asian Huns who followed the Danube into central Europe. They camped for half a century before plague sent them back to Asia in 455. Celtic tribes along the entire Danube had fled before the Huns whenever they could. Visigoths and Vandals were the first to flee. Ostrogoths (East Goths) did not get away in time and remained vassals of the Huns in their Gothic homeland at the mouth of the Danube. In central Europe, some Angles and Saxons fled to England while other Saxons and Thuringians became subjects of the Huns during their central European bivouac.

These are a few of the tribes who shifted during the *Völkerwanderung*, which lasted for centuries. Actually, tribes and peoples have wandered throughout time as the Indo-Euros did when they spread from India to Ireland. Today migration is more on an individual rather than a tribal basis.

Meroveus (sometimes spelled Merovech) led the Franks across the Rhine to escape into Gaul. He then led them into alliance with the Romans. For permission to remain in Roman territory, they became *foederati* and agreed to fight for Rome against Atilla the Hun, ca. 450.

Meroveus gave his name to the Merovingian Dynasty, which emerged with his grandson Clovis. When only fifteen years old, Clovis became chieftain and began the conquest of Gaul from the Rhine through the Loire Valley to Aquitaine as far as the Garonne Valley.

Clovis was baptized into the Roman Church in 495. As king, his conversion included the whole tribe of Franks. This gave the Franks an advantage over the Visigoths, who had converted to Arianism. So when the Franks ousted the heretic Visigoths from southern Gaul, they had the support of local clergy and the pope.

When firmly established in his new realm, Clovis transferred the Roman imperial estates to his dynasty. The Franks became Latinized during the three-century reign of the Merovingians, 450–750.

Meanwhile, back in Italy, Ostrogoths, who were finally free from the departing Huns, left their Danube homeland. Theodoric's father obtained *foederati* rights to settle in Roman territory. To see that the father lived up to his agreement, Theodoric was held hostage (from age seven to seventeen) by Zeno in Constantinople. When the father died, Theodoric returned to lead the tribe. He was well trained during his hostage days and believed he had a mandate from Zeno to set up a kingdom in Italy.

In the process of establishing his kingdom, he left law and religion alone. He did not insist on the Arianism that the Goths had converted to. Instead, he concentrated on land reform for his people, who still had a strong attachment to the land. They transformed the ravished peninsula and produced a rich agrarian base that fed Italy for the first time in centuries. They even had a surplus to trade, along with manufactured goods, through ports that Theodoric improved. He also improved aqueducts, etc., but only as his lower taxes allowed. Theodoric was not sophisticated enough to function on the financial level of extravagant deficit financing, so he naively kept the economy based on honest values. The kingdom lasted from 489 to 526, when Theodoric died. No one of his caliber rose to succeed him, though many tried.

During the contending in the West, Justinian succeeded in the Roman East as an "outstanding" emperor, 527–565. He ruled gloriously and extravagantly for thirty-eight years as he bankrupted the full treasury left by his "less-outstanding" predecessor, Anastasius. In his Orthodox zeal, Justinian routed paganism and closed Greek academies as "relics of paganism." He built many churches including the Hagia Sophia in Constantinople. His revision of the Roman law code was actually his most outstanding achievement.[1]

Justinian sought to bring the rest of Christendom into the Orthodox fold. He conquered North Africa, Southern Spain, and Southern Italy, but his twenty-year attempt to conquer the rest of Italy and replace Roman Catholicism with his Eastern Orthodoxy exhausted the east and the remnants of the Ostrogothic kingdom in Italy.

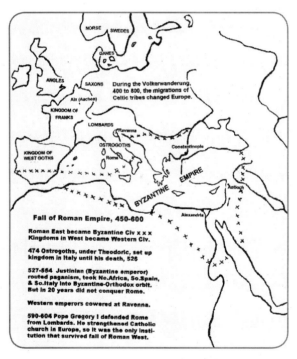

During the Volkerwanderung, 400 to 800, the migrations of Celtic tribes changed Europe.

Fall of Roman Empire, 450-600

Roman East became Byzantine Civ x x x
Kingdoms in West became Western Civ.

474 Ostrogoths, under Theodoric, set up kingdom in Italy until his death, 526

527-564 Justinian (Byzantine emperor) routed paganism, took No.Africa, So.Spain, & So.Italy into Byzantine-Orthodox orbit. But in 20 years did not conquer Rome.

Western emperors cowered at Ravenna.

590-604 Pope Gregory I defended Rome from Lombards. He strengthened Catholic church in Europe, so it was the only institution that survived fall of Roman West.

---

1. Justinian produced an encyclopedic *Corpus of Civil Law*, containing 1) *codes*, a collection of edicts; 2) *digest*, interpretations; 3) *institute*, a summary for instruction; and 4) *novellae*, new laws. He claimed that the digest revision alone reduced three million lines of law to only 150,000. (Reader's Digest Association, *Last Two Million Years*, 104). Justinian's corpus served as the basis for law in all of Western civ except Britain and the United States, whose law is Germanic, with much of it based on precedent.

Lombards came down from Germany to pick up the pieces. This was when the fourth Latin father, Gregory I, emerged to save Roman Christendom. Gregory was a Roman political official who was sent as a resident ambassador to Constantinople. He was appalled at the worldliness of the Eastern Church and reluctantly became Pope Gregory I, 590–604. He was a strong leader just when the church needed one. When has it not?

Pope Gregory saved Rome from the Lombard tribes while emperors still cowered at Ravenna and lost their power by default. Gregory then repaired the walls and aqueducts, fed the refugees, and made peace with the Lombards.

Beyond the walls of Rome, he reorganized the vast estates of the church and extended direct papal control over all clergy in Europe. All were to obey the pope and his instructions—of which he issued many. He also issued tracts on theology, saints' lives, and Benedictine rules for the monasteries. He established four monasteries from his own estates when he became pope. He added Gregorian chants and liturgy to mass. Of more dubious value, he invented purgatory as a holding place for a last chance at purification before final damnation.

Thus, the strength of the Roman Church was well established in Western Europe by the time the empire crumbled completely. In fact, the church was the only institution that survived the fall of Rome in the west.

The Orthodox Church in the Roman East followed a different path. The Eastern Church had more patriarchs than the one pope at Rome and had more translations of the Bible than the one unifying Latin version. Also, with stronger emperors in the east, such as Justinian, the church had less influence but more affluence. So the Roman East went on to enjoy nearly a thousand years of glory as the Byzantine civilization while Western civilization slowly began to emerge.

Islamic Civilization

Just as Pope Gregory solidified the administration of the Roman Church in Western Europe, a new religion emerged in the old Medi-East: Islam.

Mohammed was born in Mecca in 570. At twenty-five, he went to work for a rich widow whom he married. Until the age of forty, he managed her business and made trips to trade cities where he came in contact with Jews and Christians. On month-long meditations, he compared the one God of Judaism and Christianity with the pantheons of gods and idols the Arabs still worshipped. The angel Gabriel showed Mohammed that it was time to move on to one universal God.

For a people just abandoning their pantheons of gods, Mohammed chose the entry level into spiritual evolution that was the same as theirs. This was the time when Abraham and the Hebrews first grasped monotheism, the one-God concept. God Almighty. El Shaddai. God the Creator. So Mohammed went back to Father Abraham to found Islam.

A scholar once remarked that Islam came later in chronological time than Christianity, so it must supersede Christianity. While it came later in time, Islam began at the earlier level of spiritual development that had taken place about 2,500 years earlier in the Judeo-Christian chain of spiritual evolution. Islam has not yet worked through the long process of spiritual evolution since that entry level. In contrast to this, Reformed Christianity has worked through the entire Judeo-Christian process and has added continuing spiritual reform.

Mohammed accepted Abraham, the father of Ishmael by Hagar. (Arabs are descendants of Ishmael). Mohammed accepted the Pentateuch but rejected Judaic law because of its legalisms. He accepted Christ as a prophet second only to himself, the greatest and last prophet. He rejected Christianity because of the confusions of the Trinity. He proclaimed all men brothers under one God, Allah. Actually, that meant all Muslims were brothers. Jews and Christians, who saw half the truth, were tolerated as second-class citizens (half-brothers?). Slaves were not to be converted, for then they had to be treated as brothers and could not be used as slaves. Later on, some were converted but remained slaves.

Conversions were slow at first. Merchants in Mecca did not want to lose profits from pagan pilgrimages, so they forced Mohammed to leave. His flight to Medina, the Hegira, in 622 is year 1 of the Muslim era. Mohammed converted Medina and enough Beduoin tribesmen for an army of ten thousand. He returned to Mecca and shattered three hundred pagan idols in the Kaaba but left the sacred black stone (perhaps a meteorite). His laws wisely included a once-a-lifetime pilgrimage to Mecca in the basic five.

The five pillars are the following:

1. One God, Allah
2. Daily prayer times
3. Fast month of Ramadan
4. Alms for the poor
5. Pilgrimage to Mecca

Another handy fundamental law was the belief that the surest way to paradise was to die fighting in the cause of Allah. With these laws and the Bedouin tribesmen, conversions quickened: half of Arabia before Mohammed's death in 632, from Spain to India by 732. The most far-flung empire and widespread conversions the world had ever seen!

The vast Islamic empire was used to transfer knowledge. The Arabs had a proverb: "The ink of scholars is more precious than the blood of martyrs."[2]

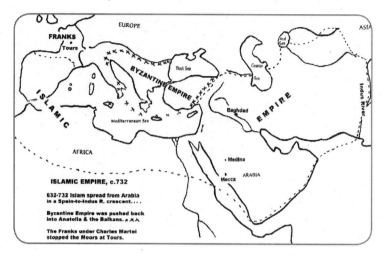

ISLAMIC EMPIRE, c.732

632-732 Islam spread from Arabia in a Spain-to-Indus R. crescent....

Byzantine Empire was pushed back into Anatolia & the Balkans.

The Franks under Charles Martel stopped the Moors at Tours.

The fund of knowledge they added to or preserved for mankind's accumulation included Greek thought, Indic math, science, and medicine. Algebra was invented in Khiva in central Asia and added to India's contribution of arabic numbers, the concept of zero, and other math. Also, the transfer of crafts and agricultural techniques from the Indus to Spain was made. Spain, with eastern style terracing and irrigation, became a garden of vineyards as never before or since. Spain also profited from more advanced metallurgy techniques. All of this industry, plus other endeavors, assured a healthy economy with wealth for Islamic caliphs and for rulers at Baghdad.

The Baghdad court became exceedingly opulent. One court reception welcomed Byzantine envoys. The palace was hung

---

2. The Arab proverb and information about the court reception came from a *National Geographic* article that has been lost.

with 22,000 Persian rugs and gilded curtains while 100 lions and 160,000 cavalrymen paraded, plus much more.

No wonder historian Ibn Khaldun proposed the first rise-fall theory of civilization. Nomads accustomed to hard living produced a rise, while the corruption of luxury and softness destined a fall, which Ibn Khaldun felt imminent.

Nomadic Seljuk and Ottoman Turks did revive Islamic civilization in thirteenth and fourteenth centuries. But the peak reached by Islamic civilization during 800 and 900 was long past by then.

Carolingian Franks

Islamic envoys, who visited Europe while Islamic civ was at its peak (ca. 800), looked with scorn on the Frankish king still "dabbling in the art of writing one's own name." Charlemagne did carry a slate on which he practiced writing his name, but he was probably helping to invent the new Carolingian script in which the letters of words were connected for the first time. Also, upper and lowercase letters were used, and punctuation was added. This was done so that more words could be squeezed onto each precious sheepskin of parchment and still be legible. The many books copied to long-lasting parchment helped save them.

The supply of papyrus from Egypt was cut off with the Islamic capture of Alexandria in 650 and control of the west Mediterranean by 670. Shiploads of spices and goods that came from India via Egypt stopped coming. Commerce dwindled to sackfuls that came by caravan through Constantinople, which absorbed most of the goods for itself. Fewer sackfuls reached Western Europe. Cities declined. Learning declined.

The *civitas* existence of classical civilization ceased because the cities ceased. People were forced out of the cities to begin anew at a down-to-earth agrarian root level. While at the very depths of this dark age and rather isolated from other civilizations, Western civilization would take form.

By God's providence so Western civ could take shape with less influence from other more sophisticated civilizations? Probably. Because in this way, the new civilization had to experience all the stages of social evolution. Also, because in this way, the Roman Church, the only institution that survived the Roman fall, would provide the central theme and driving thrust of its development. The church, under Gregory I, laid the church-state foundation of Western civ. Now the Carolinians, together with the church, would erect the frame for Western civ as it expanded into the rest of Europe.

Who were the Carolingians?[3] They were named for Charlemagne, whose ancestors were mayors of the palace under the Merovingians. *Palace* was the court, not a building. *Mayors of the palace* were like prime ministers and managed the affairs of the Merovingian court as they gradually assumed power.

Charles Martel, Charlemagne's grandfather, was the one who finally stopped the Moors at Tours. Or the Saracens at Poitiers in 732. He ousted them from most of France and adopted their new war technology—the stirrup. Then he turned to central Europe and conquered the Thuringians. They converted to Christianity under St. Boniface.

Charlemagne's father, Pepin III, reclaimed more territory from the Moors in Southern France. In Italy, he took Ravenna from the Lombards. Ravenna was supposed to be returned to the Byzantines of the old Roman East. Instead, Pepin "donated" Ravenna to the pope. As Pepin passed the document of donation, he slyly inquired, "Should title not go to him who holds the power?" The pope agreed and instructed St. Boniface to anoint Pepin king of the Franks. Thus, divine right was added to the hereditary right of kings. (It would be another one thousand years

---

3.   Friedrich Heer, *Charlemagne and His World* (New York: MacMillan Pub. Co., 1975).

before the American Declaration of Independence abolished the divine right of kings or governments.)

The Carolingian Dynasty replaced the Merovingian. Hand in hand with the church, Carolinians under Charlemagne conquered and converted much of the rest of Europe to Christianity—from the Spanish March at the Pyrenees to the Eastern March at the Balkans. (The marches were buffer zones at each end of Charlemagne's empire.)

Charlemagne took his divine right quite seriously during his half century of rule, 768–14. First he secured his title from his brother. Then he secured his capital against the Saxons. It was a thirty-year ordeal because their chief, Widukind, escaped to Denmark during the summer offensives and returned in fall after Charlemagne left. The feisty Saxons were finally conquered and forced to convert, 787. Charlemagne added most of Italy to his kingdom and received the iron crown of the Lombards from the pope. The rest of Germany was conquered and converted—by choice, not force this time. He reached Eastern Europe and the Balkans where Indo-Euro Slavs and Asiatic Bulgars and Avars were pushing west. He contained them in the Eastern March.

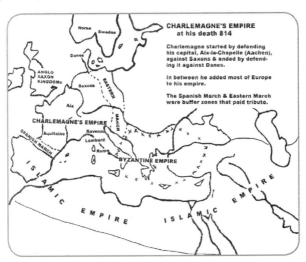

Charlemagne ended his reign as he began it, by fighting to defend his capital at Aix la Chapelle (now Aachen). First he fought the neighboring Saxons. At the end, he fought the Danes who were part of the Scandinavian expansion, which grew with the onset of a five-century warming trend. By then, Charlemagne was an old man of seventy. The Danes exhausted him. He was carried back on a litter and died in 814.

Much transpired between his first and final defense of the capital, Aix la Chapelle. Charlemagne built a stone palace with a chapel copied from one in Ravenna. (Chapels were places to keep Christian "relics.") He built other palaces at strategic locations in the empire, such as Regensburg on the Danube at its most northern point. He started a canal between the Rhine and Danube to tie his empire together. He built a navy in the North Sea and in the Adriatic.

Charlemagne's most lasting contributions were in education. He brought scholars to the palace school headed by Alcuin from York. Theodulf the Goth from Spain was the court theologian. In his writings, Theodulf defended *filioque*, the Son, which put Christ on the same level as the Father and Holy Spirit in the Trinity.[4]

Charlemagne also ordered that parish schools actually teach and that cathedral schools be established to fill the gap between the parish and monastery. He ordered that the priesthood be reformed according to instructions of Pope Hadrian, who worked with Charlemagne for twenty years while he was pope. With all of this, plus Carolingian script and musical notation, rudimentary foundations were laid in 800 that produced the renaissance of 1200, when many cathedral schools became universities.

We often underestimate the importance of such basic foundations, which are a necessary part of the pre-civ stage of

---

4. Ibid., 162.

development. This stage must undergird a society before real civilization can flourish and flower. Charlemagne has been mistakenly underestimated in this area of education because these basic steps are not fully appreciated.

Charlemagne has also been faulted for not initiating primogeniture among the heirs to his throne. Actually, he planned quite well for his succession, but plans go oft awry. Eldest son, Charles, at Aix la Chapelle, was trained to rule the empire but died unexpectedly. Son Pepin was trained to rule Italy but died in an Adriatic Sea battle in 810. Charlemagne came back on the litter from fighting the Danes and died at seventy in 814. Only Louis was left.

Louis was trained to administer a province, Aquitaine. He never grasped the idea of empire and ignored the advisors in Aix la Chapelle who did. He spent most of his twenty-five-year reign settling the succession of his sons: Charles in France, Louis in Germany, and Lothar in Italy, who was to rule the empire. So a corridor was designed from Italy to the capital at Aix la Chapelle. It was known as *Lotharii regni* or Lothar's reign, then Lotharingia, and finally, Lorraine. But Lothar died, so Charles and Louis—France and Germany—fought over Lorraine for years, until World War I in 1914.

East Frankish Empire as HRE

Grandson Louis ruled his east Frankish empire (Germany) from the castle Charlemagne built at Regensburg. Louis received the region east of that fateful corridor to Aix. This included Saxony, Bavaria, and part of the Eastern March (The buffer area in Eastern Europe).

His realm in north central Europe was spared the invasions of the Scandinavian Norse and Swedes that occurred in northwest and northeast Europe. Saxon strength may have been the deterrent.

The Saxons, who gave Charlemagne so much trouble, were finally assimilated and brought new vigor to the east Franks. One of their lords, Otto the Saxon, married the great-granddaughter of Louis the German. Her lineage did not really count except for prestige. Their son, Henry the Fowler, was elected king of Germany by the nobles in 919. After the last male heir of Louis died, the nobles returned to the age-old custom of electing the strongest duke to rule the independent duchies.

Henry's strength was needed to defeat the Magyars, a new group of Asian invaders akin to the Avars. In the process of pursuing the Magyars, who raided as far as the left bank of the Rhine, Henry naturally added the Rhine area to his duchy. This included Lorraine (the heart of Charlemagne's empire) and added to the power and prestige Henry bequeathed to his son Otto.

Otto was easily elected king as Henry's successor in 936. Otto immediately made the church his ally, for the church was the only other power that superseded duchy bounds. Otto made favorable appointments of the higher clergy in Germany, although Roman nobles still selected the pope.

Otto expanded his power into Italy by marrying the widow of the deceased king of the Lombards. He became king of the Lombards in 951 but was opposed by Lombard nobles who stirred up trouble. The pope, who feared Lombard unity, called Otto back in 961 to settle the trouble. In return, the pope crowned him Otto I, emperor of the Holy Roman Empire, and gave him the privilege of confirming papal elections. Roman nobles objected and ousted Otto's pope. Otto returned and reseated his choice. Reousted! Reseated! Otto finally won.

Sandwiched between Otto's trips to Italy were battles with the Magyars. Otto routed the Magyars from Moravia, after which Moravia and its overlord, Bohemia, became vassals of the Holy Roman Empire. During this period, Moravia and Bohemia turned to the west, whereas they had been in the Byzantine orbit before. Magyars finally settled among their distant Avar kin. Together with the Slavs, they became the westernized Roman Catholic country of Hungary.

EUROPE, c.1000
Holy Roman Empire of Otto's
Saxon Dynasty • • • • • •
Normans opened Mediterranean
and started Crusades when they
took Sicily & South Italy

Scandinavian Expansion

The west Frankish empire of Charles followed a different course as it, and most of Western Europe, were changed by Scandinavian invasions.

Five centuries of warm weather (800 to 1300) benefitted Scandinavian exploration and expansion. Good weather meant good crops, even two a year, with an increase in population. Invigorated Scandinavians sent even more groups than usual in search of new territory. Vikings sailed to Iceland and Greenland, where they established colonies.[5] Lief Ericson reached North America around 1000. The return of cold weather forced them to abandon Greenland. Iceland survived and preserved the legendary history in the Eddas.

In northeast Europe, Swedes established trading posts at Novgorod and Kiev on their Baltic-to-Balkan route to Constantinople.[6] They also set up a trading post at Moscow. These became city-states ruled by Scandinavian nobility, who adopted Eastern Orthodox Christianity during their trips to Constantinople; Moscow, in 988.

The Danes, who plagued Charlemagne, also raided and settled the east coast of England. They demanded "Danegeld" to stop inland raids. Danes also settled in Ireland at Dublin, Waterford, and Limerick, where they were assimilated and converted to Celtic Christianity. Strangely, or perhaps providentially, the eleventh century produced a renaissance in religion, literature, and the arts as monks sought to preserve the ancient traditions. They diligently copied old manuscripts and also recorded the scripts of old languages.

Between the Danes and the Norse, who settled at the mouth of the Seine, Charlemagne's successors gave up and told the people to find a lord to protect them. Feudalism by decree was followed by the complete collapse of the Carolingians in France. The Capets of Paris stopped the Norse in their raids up the Seine. They replaced the Carolingians when Hugh Capet was elected to

---

5. Vikings were named from the viks, inlets, and fjords of the North and Baltic Seas. They sailed in seventy- to eighty-foot, flat-bottomed boats similar to those described by Caesar, except oarsmen were added.

6. Goods of trade were packed on rafts for the Elbe-Oder-Danube route of Baltic-to-Balkan trade with Byzantine Constantinople. When Huns occupied the Danube, the Dnieper route to the Black Sea was opened with trading posts along the route. Amber was an item of trade. Also food, fur, textiles, jewelry, iron ore, metal goods.

rule France in 997. The Capets wisely increased their power over time, which they did not waste in useless wars.

The Carolingians had already ceded "Normandy" to the Norse when Hrolf (or Rollo) converted to Christianity for permission to stay in 911. Incensed Frankish nobles immediately built a ring of castles to keep the Norse in Normandy. By the end of the century, Normandy became the best organized province in France and ready to expand, but certainly not at the expense of their Frankish overlords. Why not England where Scandinavians were spreading paganism? William of Normandy, with the pope's blessing and the promise of England as a papal fief, sailed across the channel to conquer England in 1066.

William landed in Kent just as Harold of England defeated Harold Hardrada of Norway, who tried to establish himself at York. The English Harold hurried from York to Hastings and to his own defeat. He was shot by a bowman as William's knights fought to chants of the Roland epic.[7] From a toehold in Kent, William began his conquests, which he secured with castles—like the ring the Franks had erected around Normandy. The new castles and territory were parceled among William's nobles who, as alien conquerors, remained exceedingly loyal to their benefactor.

Within a century of William's conquest, his grandson Henry II tried to repeat his feat. In 1155, Henry received Pope Adrian's blessing and the promise of Ireland as a papal fief if he brought order to the church and state in Ireland. In 1166, Henry sent Welch lords to liberate Dublin, Waterford, and Limerick from Danish control, even though the Danes were already assimilated.

---

7. The Roland epic was handed down as a chant from 778 when Charlemagne (or his grandfather, Charles Martel) led a foray into Spain. Roland's wagon train of provisions fell behind the rear guard and was attacked while filing through a pass. It was destroyed in spite of Roland's valiant efforts, which were remembered in chants not committed to writing until after Hastings.

Nevertheless, the king of Leinster was deposed, and a Welsh lord claimed the Leinster crown by marrying his daughter.

Rory O'Connor, king of Connaught, tried to rescue Ireland by pushing the invaders back into Dublin. Henry himself brought an army to Waterford to relieve the forces in Dublin. In 1172, all of Ireland paid homage to Henry, except Connaught and Ulster, which Rory saved.[8] Henry brought order to state and church by making them subject to England through Henry's feudal overlords. Ireland would never be the same yet would never change. The agri-craft economy based on oats, barley, flax, and linen, dairying, and glass production would never change; but their long history of civilization would be denigrated and erased, except for those recopied manuscripts forgotten and all but lost in the monasteries.

"Order" would be fought over for centuries. When Henry VIII separated the Church of England from the Roman Catholic in 1541, the Irish reasoned that the papal fiefdom was no longer in force. So Ireland was independent again. England did not follow this line of reasoning and kept Ireland as a political vassal, if not a religious one.

Normans Reopen the Mediterranean

Just a few decades after William left Normandy to conquer England, Robert Guiscard left for the Mediterranean. His expedition was as timely as William's. Islamic unity had disintegrated into rivalry between the caliphs. Seljuk Turks usurped control in Baghdad in 1055 while other Seljuks battled

---

8. The "fifths" of Ireland were much like the four now. Clockwise, they are 1) Munster in the south, 2) Connaught in the west, 3) Ulster in the northeast (now Northern Ireland), and 4) Leinster in the east central area around Dublin.

Byzantine Orthodox Christians in Anatolia. With all of that for diversion, Guiscard timed his Mediterranean expedition rather well in 1080.

Guiscard easily took South Italy from Byzantine control and immediately applied to the pope for recognition. The pope knew that South Italy in the papal orbit was preferable to nominal Byzantine control and the Orthodox orbit. He quickly recognized South Italy as Norman territory in exchange for the promise of homage, plus Norman support against both the Lombards and the Holy Roman emperor.

In 1091, with Italy as a base, the Normans conquered Islamic Sicily. It became a Norman kingdom with the capital at Palermo, when the pope crowned Guiscard's nephew king in 1131. For centuries, Sicily was the most enlightened and best-governed state in Europe.

Historians often marvel at the way barbarians impose their rule on decaying civilization and rejuvenate it. The barbarians were probably well into the pre-civ stage in order to mount their invasion in the first place. The Norse reached that point way back in Scandinavia. After adopting from Frankish culture in Normandy, they were able to appreciate the benefits of advanced civilization by the time they reached Islamic Sicily. They certainly appreciated Sicily as a strategic location to continue their seafaring and trade.

Perhaps the quality of Islamic civilization has also been underestimated. It was in many ways superior to anything Europe had ever produced, including Greco-Roman. Although Sicily was in deep decline, a vigorous people rejuvenated it at just the right time. Norman Sicily quickly became the most remarkable state in Europe, and Palermo was second only to Constantinople.

The Normans unwittingly launched the Crusades when they reopened the Mediterranean. Western civilization would soon reach its Gothic peak.

Gothic Middle Ages

In round numbers, the turn of the millennium at 1000 marked the beginning of a new age: the Middle Ages. The Medieval or Gothic period. It was distinguished for the building of cathedrals and the launching of crusades.

The Gothic cathedral was symbolic of the age, for the unity of design and unity of purpose that built the cathedral expressed the *unity of society* and its highest ideal: *unity with God*, who was at the center of their universe.

> The Gothic style with pointed arches took weight off walls…flying buttresses strengthened the walls so arches could soar…space between the ribs was opened with stained glass windows or was filled with Biblical figures beautifully and honestly wrought, even in the topmost finial that no eye could see…The best that a craftsman could give in the service of his religion was amazingly accomplished with primitive tools…built over a half or a few centuries, a cathedral with soaring arches aspired toward heaven as men aspired toward heaven. Men of the middle ages in the springtime of their religious fervor built the cathedral—not for their God, He was in heaven, but for themselves—to worship Him…Their Gothic cathedral came alive when thronged with worshippers, with organ pealing, choir singing, light streaming in stained glass windows…It was a harmonious whole and magnificent setting for expression of the common faith of an entire people…A universal church! A universal society![9]

Holy Roman emperor Otto III was caught up in this same religious fervor and unity of high purpose. He initiated moral

---

9. Stewart C. Easton, *The Heritage of Past: Earliest Times to 1500* (New York: Holt, Rineheart and Winston, 1964), 657–661.

THE RIGHT HAND OF GOD

and spiritual reform by appointing reform popes. Pope Sylvester, educated in Spain, was too far ahead of his time to effect any change in his four short years as pope, 999–1003. Otto appointed other reform popes, who were too moral to cater to emperors. So the Saxon dynasty was replaced by the Franconian (Salian) Henrys, 1036–1122, who continued the HRE Henry numbers with Henry III. They also continued to appoint clergy and popes.

In 1056, Henry III died, leaving his six-year-old son, Henry IV, as emperor and his wife as regent. The papacy, with Hildebrand as advisor, sought to strengthen its position during the regency period, especially enough to elect its own popes. Hildebrand became Pope Gregory VII in 1073. By then, Henry IV was grown and ready to assume his throne and his right to appoint clergy. Gregory opposed Henry's appointments. Henry deposed the pope. Gregory dethroned Henry; then he started on a trip to Germany to rally the nobles to elect Henry's successor.

Gregory stopped at Canossa in Tuscany. Henry came in sackcloth and barefoot in the snow to beg forgiveness. The pope, as priest, could not refuse forgiveness, or he would lose morale and spiritual support and authority in Western Christendom. Neither could he forgive and reinstate Henry, or he would lose political authority. The priestly-political dilemma unnerved Gregory for the rest of his papacy, which Henry quickly ended after he settled the aroused nobles, convened the German clergy, deposed the pope, and installed his own in 1084. Gregory fled to Monte Casino and soon died.

The next popes launched the Crusades. The First Crusade of 1095 was called by Pope Urban II to regain Anatolia for the Byzantine Empire. Urban II promised "plenary indulgence," a sort of total forgiveness that guaranteed salvation without purgatory to anyone who died fighting for the cause. Fifty thousand people went to Constantinople, where the emperor shipped them across the Bosporus to be massacred by Muslims.

The military part of the crusade got off in 1099 when Norman, Italian, German, and French knights captured Jerusalem, Edessa, Antioch, and surrounding territory. Little was returned to the Byzantines. Europe profited instead—especially Venice, Genoa, and Pisa—who sent supply ships that returned with oriental goods of trade.

In Spain, the marquises of the Spanish March (the buffer zone between the Franks and the Moors of Spain) became kings and expanded their kingdoms from the Pyrenees into Muslim territory. By 1150, the four kingdoms of Navarre, Portugal, Aragon, and Leon-Castile reclaimed half of the Iberian Peninsula. By 1490, Granada was the only Muslim area left. Granada was reclaimed in 1492—a more important event in Spanish history than the discovery of America that same year.

The Crusade of 1190 was launched to recapture losses to the brilliant Muslim general Saladin, especially Jerusalem. This crusade affected Europe the most. The pope called the crusade to get the three most powerful men *in* Europe *out* of Europe.

Holy Roman Emperor Frederick I ("Barbarossa," "red beard" in Italian) died en route.[10] By then, his son Henry VI was married to a Norman princess, Constance. The marriage united the HRE of the north (Germany) with Norman South Italy and Sicily. Henry VI died, so his son Frederick II inherited the whole empire while he was only a child of three. The pope made himself regent for Fred II.

---

10. The title of *Holy Roman Emperor* passed from Saxon Ottos (919–1036), to Franconian Henrys, (1036–1122), to Hohenstaufen Fredericks as influence and dynasties moved south. Each dynasty had a few significant Henrys and continued the numbering. Henry the Fowler added Rhine-Lorraine to Saxon HRE. Franconian Henry IV unnerved Gregory VII. Hohenstaufen Henry VI united the HRE with Norman Italy and Sicily though his marriage to Constance.

The second powerful man the pope wanted *out* of Europe was Philip II of France. Philip abandoned the crusade and went back to reunite his country and to regain English territory in Normandy, Aquitaine, and other parts of France while Richard I of England was off to lionhearted glory in the Holy Land. Richard, the third powerful ruler, did not abandon the crusade. He secured Acre and Jaffa but knew he could not recapture Jerusalem and hold it. In September 1192, Richard and Saladin made a truce. Christians kept the coastal towns. Saladin kept Jerusalem, but Christians were given permission to enter the city. In October 1192, Richard returned to England.

Richard now faced the problems Philip of France launched when he returned to reunite France and regain territory from England. Richard died in battle in Europe in 1199. Brother John then had to fight Philip. John was joined by the duke of Flanders and Otto of Swabia, who wanted the HRE throne instead of young Frederick II. The Battle of Bouvines in 1214 was one of the crucial battles of history. Philip won. The losers were John, Otto, and the duke of Flanders.

Pope Innocent III presided at the peace. He gave Philip the English territory in France. He intended to give England itself to France but gave Flanders instead—after John pledged England as a vassal state in order to keep his crown. English nobles did not like the idea of being vassals to the pope. A year later, 1215, they forced John to sign the Magna Carta, which limited the king's power.

Pope Innocent III (1198–1216), who was anything but innocent, had stirred up strife between contenders for the HRE throne after Henry died. Now he excommunicated and deposed Otto of Swabia. Then he proclaimed his protégé, Fred II, as Holy Roman emperor because he thought he could control the young Frederick.

Papal political power was at its peak. Innocent III extended political control over most of Europe, also over the Byzantine Empire, which became a vassal state after crusaders sacked Constantinople in 1204. Venetians may have inspired the sack. Genoa, rival of Venice, restored a Byzantine emperor half a century later.

The Crusades now turned against "heretic" Christians when the biggest threat came from the Mongols. Genghis Khan swept through Asia and devastated Islamic territory as far as Baghdad. He shattered Kiev and much of Eastern Europe. Moscow was spared and ready to expand after they left. Khans brought nothing (not even algebra) to the lands they conquered. However, they did invite emissaries and missionaries to bring outside ideas to Peiping. The Khans were shopping for a new religion. Muslims sent emissaries with success, but the papacy was more interested in controlling Europe while few priests were interested in the hardships of a trip east.

An opportunity lost? Maybe. Or maybe God planned to send reformed Christianity to the West, to the New World, instead.

Marco Polo did journey to China from Venice at the end of the century, ca. 1298. Later, in a Genoese prison, he related his trip to a fellow prisoner. The book of his adventures was popular in Europe. It probably helped launch another Genoese on his trip to the West and to the New World two centuries later.

Gothic Peak and Plummet

In the meantime, Holy Roman Emperor Frederick II brought new ideas to Europe. These he absorbed while being reared and educated in the Sicily of his Norman mother, Constance. Remember, Palermo was the greatest and richest city in Europe after Constantinople.

Because of his Sicilian background, Frederick was probably the best educated ruler in Europe. He may have introduced arabic numbers to Europe. He understood the importance of a sound economic base to his kingdom. He built a fleet to encourage trade, industry, and prosperity, which he then could tax. His Sicilian revenues and Muslim recruits, who were immune to papal influence, kept his armies in the field.

The first use of his armies was to honor the crusade debt he owed for being crowned holy Roman emperor in 1220. By 1227, Pope Gregory IX pressured Frederick with threats of excommunication, then actual excommunication. This was partly so that the pope's mercenaries could take South Italy while Fred II was out of the country, and the excommunicated ruler's territory was up for grabs.

But Fred returned all too soon. In contact with Islam all his life and fluent in Arabic (also German, Latin, Greek), Frederick simply invited the sultan of Egypt, the overlord of Palestine, to negotiate with him. Without swinging a sword, Frederick got most of Jerusalem, Nazareth, Bethlehem, a strip of coast, and a ten-year truce.

Frederick quickly returned and ousted the pope's mercenaries. He reorganized South Italy and Sicily. He established the University of Naples to train administrators for his kingdoms. He planned to reorganize the rest of the Holy Roman Empire, North Italy, and Germany, where his son Conrad ruled. But the papacy did not want the papal states sandwiched between a strong united HRE, so the pope stirred the Lombard League of cities to resist him.

Frederick urged other kings to join him. After all, he was fighting their battle too so that national unity could supersede the power of city-states. Evidently, no one understood, for no one helped. Frederick was killed battling the Lombards. His son died. His grandson was murdered.

Italy and Germany were destined to become fragmented city-states and principalities because the papacy destroyed anyone with power enough to unite the empire. Pro-empire Ghibellines and anti-empire Guelphs battled for centuries. Dante remarked that even a German Ghibelline was preferable to the chaos that ensued.

HOLY ROMAN EMPIRE, 1250
- - - - HREmpire of Frederic II
Lombard League Cities:
1 Milan, 2 Turin, 3 Genoa, 4 Pisa,
5 Florence, 6 Bologna, 7 Padua
o o o o Claimed by Papacy

Anjou of France added to the chaos. Since Frederick's illegitimate son Manfred could not inherit his Norman territory, the pope gave it to Anjou, brother of the French king. Anjou fought for years to claim his "gift." In revenge for Anjou's ravishing abuse of the Sicilians, every Frenchman in Sicily was killed in the Sicilian Vespers. Finally, Sicily went to Spain through the marriage of Manfred's daughter into the house of Aragon. Their descendant, Ferdinand of Aragon, married Isabella of Castile to unite Spain.

The papacy became a pawn of the French king and moved to Avignon near the mouth of the Rhone in 1305. When Pope Gregory XI returned to Rome and died there, popes were elected in both Rome and Avignon. Kings aligned behind the two popes. Schism fractured Europe. As each pope excommunicated adherents of the other, schism fractured the souls of people. It lasted forty years, 1378 to 1417, but never really healed.

The Gothic period, which began at the millennium with unity of spirit and society, reached its peak under Frederick II in the thirteenth century then plummeted so quickly in the fourteenth that everything was shattered. Society! Spirit! Everything!

God was still in his heaven—perhaps—but certainly not here on earth with His people. Dante's *Inferno* enveloped the living. Black plague entered Europe when infested rats jumped ship in Palermo in 1347. It also came in caravans from the East. Plague quickly spread and killed more than a third of the population between India and Ireland in two years. The cold of the Little Ice Age, after five warm centuries, diminished the crops and brought famine, which weakened people. The Baltic Sea froze twice during the first years of 1300. Plague returned four more times during the century. Europe's booming population of the preceding balmy centuries was cut in half to thirty million.

As labor became scarce, peasants and burghers scraped together the money to purchase their freedom. Serfs became uneconomic because they had to be fed precious food and so were given their freedom. In spite of the labor shortage, manufacturing did not lag—thanks to labor-saving innovations of the past two centuries such as the windmill, watermill, compass with pivoting needle, clock, spinning wheel, and treadle loom. The same amount of goods spread among fewer people meant a higher standard of living for all.

The clergy and nobility had an exceedingly high standard with many special privileges, even though they failed to tend to the spiritual or military needs of the people. Brigands terrorized Europe as the Hundred Years' War between France and England continued. Crusades became exercises in futility with many aimed against "heretic" Christians. Now in lieu of a crusade or pilgrimage to the Holy Land, monetary contributions could be made for the indulgence of a purgatory bypass. With the sale of indulgences, the church grew ever more wealthy and corrupt but did nothing for the people. Yet it turned against heretics who cried for reform.

The outmoded three-estate social system was not changed to account for the growing middle class, who were regarded as third-estate commoners. Even though clergy and nobles of the first and second estate failed in their duties to the people, the clergy remained exempt from taxes, and nobles were partly exempt. Tithes and taxes fell on the people. Hearth tax. Sales tax. Wine tax. Salt tax. Consumption tax. Plus the worst tax of all, inflation and devalued money. Most taxes went to finance the wars of family feuds between the nobility because marriage, divorce, and cousinships determined borders rather than the natural interests of the people.

Besides the outmoded social-political system, outmoded economic ideas also persisted in the fourteenth century. These were reinforced by religious concepts that never should have been the mode. Although economic thinking was just past the agri-craft barter level, the "theo-logic" used to classify commerce and finance as "mortal sin" is unfathomable. The commerce of middle-class merchants was condemned but could be forgiven for a fee. The more deadly sins of moneylending and usury were left to the Jews because they were damned anyway. By the same sort of strange illogic, the overborrowing of money that resulted in huge deficits and bankruptcy was blamelessly pure, especially if it financed senseless largesse or incessant war.

Battle brought honor and glory, even salvation, if declared a crusade by the papacy. The pope could dispense or withhold salvation at whim, as if by turning a spigot on or off. When schism brought two popes to their thrones, 1378–1417, salvation really flowed hot and cold.

At a time when values and ideas are so completely at odds with sanity and reality, crisis is bound to ensue, which will overturn the idiocy. The irony of fate, if nothing else, is the wry a righting of the awry. As the fourteenth century turned to fifteenth, such a crisis period of righting began. Not because the powers-that-be came to their senses but in spite of them! Because the providence of history and the underlying law of balance prevails in the end. However, mankind, with its after-the-fact politics, can do a very effective job of tipping the scales to delay balance, thereby causing more pain than necessary.

Gothic society was shattered and changing. The medieval ideal of the unity of society was to be replaced with the unity of the person. Inevitably but painfully, reform would finally evolve.

Steps to Reform

Early Gothic thinkers started the reform. They laid thought upon thought—as cathedral masons laid stone upon stone—until a staircase of steps carried at least part of Christendom over the Reformation threshold.

Although abstract ideas and formal logic were discovered by Thales of Ionia (600 BC) and used by Paul in his New Testament reasoning, they now impacted Western thought with much debate about "universals" and "particulars." Platonists held that universals had permanent reality while the particulars of earthly phenomena were only relative and inferior copies. For example,

> If 'humanity' is real, then God might have justification in
> punishing all men for the sin of Adam, who was part of

humanity. But if only individual men exist, each should be judged on his own merits and not share in the sin of Adam.[11]

Anselm of Bec and Canterbury (1034-1109) produced a "systematic theory of atonement of the Son for the sins of man, hitherto missing from Christian theology."[12]

Peter Abelard (1079–1142), better known for his unfortunate love affair with Heloise, entered the debate and sent thought in a new direction. He stated that the common element in things is discovered by the mind, and this element has its own reality, although a mental one. A concept! Through Abelard, Western civilization reached the stage where man could see and "name" abstract ideas. He no longer needed myths and stories to convey abstract ideas. He now had mental concepts with which to reason and to question everything—even theology—rather than to accept anything on blind faith. The idea of the *individual* thinking for himself began to emerge. Also, empirical thought from observation and experience (the only kind used in the Old Testament) was now "discovered" and used in science.

Individual judgment versus ecclesiastical authority began to emerge. William of Ockham, a Franciscan who died in 1349, denied papal authority in temporal matters and thought the papacy a little too absolute in spiritual, especially in interpreting the Bible as the pope and clergy saw fit.

Half the Reformation staircase was built by John Wycliffe, an Oxford theologian (1320?–1384). He denied that the church, its priests, or the pope were necessary for salvation.

For each man that shall be damned shall be damned by his own guilt, and each man that is saved shall be saved by his own merit.[13]

11. Easton, *The Heritage of Past*, 630
12. Ibid., 629
13. Barbara Tuchman, *A Distant Mirror*, p.339

Wycliffe's idea of salvation needed a little more reforming. In the meantime, he rejected excommunication, confessions, pilgrimages, worship of relics and saints, indulgences, and the treasury of merit. Instead, he offered the Bible in English. His Bible spread even though it was handwritten—and forbidden. He was executed in 1384.

John Huss (Jan Hus) echoed Wycliffe's teachings in Bohemia. In 1415, he was burned at the stake. His death ignited the Hussite Wars for vengeance and Czech independence. Hussites used new methods of warfare. They circled baggage wagons in a moving fort that withstood cavalry charges. Then with pikes, flails, canon, and the first use of handheld guns, Hussites won the war. But they were unable to overcome ideological conflicts in order to remain in power.

Savonarola (1452–1498) reformed Florence. Neither the pope, the nobles, nor the people could stand the way he dictated good and purity. So he was burned at the stake, and the Medicis returned to rule.

Joan of Arc was burned at the stake in 1428 for her part in the Hundred Year' War between France and England, which finally ended in 1453. The year 1453 was important in Europe. The war ended. Gutenberg invented movable type for the printing press. Constantinople fell to Ottoman Turks, ending Byzantine civilization. Refugees fled to Italy and inspired the Renaissance. They also introduced double-entry bookkeeping, which may have been the greater service. Merchants, bankers, and kings would finally know if they were solvent or bankrupt.

Although much lauded, the Renaissance was actually a regressive movement. The one-thousand-year foundation of Western civ was denigrated while Greek and Roman classics were resurrected. Classical Latin was a dead language ever since Jerome translated the Bible into the Latin Vulgate. This evolving living Latin was used throughout Europe in the church, universities, law, and diplomacy. It bound Europe together with a free flow of scholars and ideas. The free flow slowed with a revival of classical Latin then stopped with the literary use of national languages.

The resurrection of classical Latin would be as if we today went back to Chaucer's English, which was even older than that of Shakespeare. *Whan that Aprille with his shoures sote* (When that April with its showers sweet), etc. Rather than go back to a dead ancient Latin, writers moved on to living spoken languages. Dante wrote his *Divine Comedy* in his native Tuscan, which became the national language of Italy. Luther translated the Bible into his High German, which became the national language.

When Renaissance humanists went back to Cicero and his *humanitas* of 50 BC, humanity was soon back at the center of the universe instead of God. Scholars began to reconcile classical humanities with Christian values. This produced Christian humanism, of which Erasmus of the Netherlands gave the most popular expression of the time, thanks to his wit and printing press.

Incidentally, two decades after the fall of Constantinople in 1453, Czar Ivan of Moscow married a Byzantine princess and took the remains of Byzantine civilization to Moscow. He proclaimed Russia the protector of the Orthodox Church and Moscow the third Rome (*czar* is a contraction of *Caesar*). Poor Russia began a fateful pattern of adopting a trend when it was too late—when it was obsolete or in need of reform. Byzantine civilization was long over, and Christianity was overdue for reform.

More important than Ivan's 1479 marriage was the 1469 marriage in Spain that united Isabella of Castile and Ferdinand of Aragon. Isabella used her jewels to sponsor the voyage of a Genoese sailor, Christopher Columbus, who planned to reach the Orient by sailing west. Through the foresight of Prince Henry the Navigator, the Portuguese already sponsored voyages that sailed around Africa to reach the Orient. By strange coincidence, or providence, the Chinese fleet of the Ming Dynasty withdrew from East Africa (because of internal problems) just as the Portuguese ventured that far.

So the flow of influence was to be from the west to the east. The thrust of the future was to be through Western civilization as it moved into the world, especially into the New World. Was it an accident or providence that the New World was discovered—rather rediscovered—just in time to provide a place for Reformation refugees?

Crossing the Threshold of Reform

Martin Luther (1483–1546) was born about ten years before the discovery of America. He climbed the Reformation staircase the early Gothic thinkers built as they laid thought upon thought. Luther opened the door and crossed the threshold of Reform—after he tacked his ninety-five theses on the door of the church at Wittenberg.[14]

Luther was the son of a Thuringian mine operator who wanted him to study law so he could care for his parents in their old age. When he was twenty-two years old, Luther was caught in a thunderstorm.

He promised to give his life to God if God saved him. God did. So he felt called by God to become an Augustinian monk. His father questioned the call. "God grant it was not an apparition of the Devil." The devil and demons were very real and very active at this time of much superstition. (Luther later did away with exorcism in the Protestant Church.)

Luther became a dedicated monk at the monastery at Erfurt. A dispute in the Augustinian order was to be settled by the pope in Rome in 1510. Luther was one of two monks sent from Erfurt. In Rome, he saw the piers laid for the new stone St. Peter's Cathedral

---

14. Information on Luther from Roland Bainton, *Here I Stand* (Nashville: Abingdon Press, 1978).

that was to replace the wooden basilica. He missed seeing the antiquities of Rome and masterpieces of the Renaissance because he concentrated on shrines, relics, and bones of saints.

Relics and bones were venerated for salvation because they represented the "treasury of merit." The excess good of saints was stored in the "treasury" and dispensed through indulgences, which people bought to lessen their years in purgatory. Rome was the greatest storehouse of such treasures. One crypt had forty popes and seventy-six thousand martyrs. Rome even had the steps from Pilate's palace, which Luther climbed on hands and knees. He kissed each step and repeated a *"Pater Noster"* to save his grandparents from purgatory. At the top of the stairs, Luther questioned, "Who knows if it is so?"

Luther was appalled at the incompetence, ignorance, immorality, and frivolity of the Italian priests and the Renaissance pope Leo X, a Medici who said that God gave them the papacy to enjoy. And he did. (Catholics admit this low point in the papacy and later reformed.)

When Luther returned from Rome, he was sent to teach at Wittenberg and spent the rest of his life there. Wittenberg was a village of 2,500 people with a mile-long main street. The university was at one end, and the Augustinian cloister at the other. The university was a pet project of Frederick of Saxony. He built it to rival the century-old university at Leipzig, but it fell short. So three new teachers were called. Luther taught Psalms, Romans, and Galatians.

While studying Romans 1:16–17, Luther discovered "justification by faith." No one can *merit* salvation by his own doing. Luther realized this as a monk. Later he said that if anyone could be saved by "monkery," he should have been. He obeyed the laws, duties, study, fasting, prayers of the order, but still felt unacceptable. Unsaved. Now he saw that only faith by God's grace brought salvation. *Faith* that through Christ we are forgiven and acceptable to God!

If works and penance could not earn salvation, indulgences certainly could not buy it. Luther already concluded it was beyond reason to think the pope could deliver souls from purgatory. If he can, then he is cruel not to release them all. But Pope Leo needed money for the new St. Peter's, so Dominican monk Tetzel was sent to collect indulgences in a nearby town. Tetzel had a saying, "As soon as the coin in the coffer rings, the soul from purgatory springs."

Frederick did not allow the sale in Saxony. He had a relic collection second to Rome with five thousand items centered on a thorn from the crown that pierced Jesus's brow, a nail from the cross, a straw from the manger, a twig from Moses's bush, plus nineteen thousand bones of saints. Fred spent years amassing his collection of "all the saints" viewed for indulgences on All Saints' Day on November 1.

On Hallowed Eve (Halloween) October 31, 1517, Luther posted his "95 theses for debate" on the church door. The debate was aimed at Tetzel and the pope, not Fred of Saxony. But six years later, Fred's relics were worthless. Still he kept them.

In the debate over indulgences, Luther pointed out the mistranslation in the Latin Bible of Jerome compared to Erasmus's translation from the Greek. Erasmus translated Matthew 4:17 as "Repent for the Kingdom of God is at hand" instead of "Do penance for the kingdom of heaven is at hand." The correct translation—*repent*, which means "*be* penitent," instead of "*do* penance"—undercut the indulgences.

Dominicans backed Tetzel. Augustinians backed Luther. Debates, hearings, and trials continued in Augsburg, Leipzig, Heidelberg, and Worms. By 1519, Luther insisted that Holy Scripture was the supreme authority rather than the pope or the church. The Dominican master of the Sacred Palace at Rome upheld the doctrine of the Roman Church and Roman pontiff as "the infallible rule of faith [*from*] which sacred scripture derived strength and authority."

Luther stated, "A simple layman armed with Scripture is to be believed above a pope or council without it." This statement sanctioned and upheld the "priesthood of the believer."

Luther expected to be burned at the stake. What a disgrace to his parents. But he was lucky in his timing. He had Gutenberg's press for his many tracts and his Bible. He had Frederick of Saxony who insisted the trials be in Germany. He was also lucky the pope and emperor were too busy to really care about an insignificant friar in the hinterlands. Pope Leo X issued a papal bull (edict) condemning Luther's teachings. Luther burned the bull. Leo excommunicated Luther then returned to his pursuit of old manuscripts, art, and sculpture to fill St. Peter's and the new Vatican buildings that the indulgences paid for.

Charles V was even busier ruling his empire. His mother, Joanna, the daughter of Ferdinand and Isabella, married into the Habsburgs of Austria. The son of Joanna and Philip I became Charles I of Spain and Charles V of the Holy Roman Empire. This genealogy chart of the Habsburgs will help.

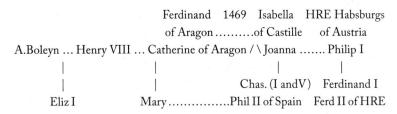

```
                    Ferdinand   1469   Isabella   HRE Habsburgs
                       of Aragon..........of Castille     of Austria
A.Boleyn ... Henry VIII ... Catherine of Aragon / \ Joanna ....... Philip I
     |                    |                    |                 |
     |                    |              Chas. (I and V)   Ferdinand I
   Eliz I               Mary................Phil II of Spain   Ferd II of HRE
```

In Europe, Charles ruled Spain, the Netherlands, Austria, Burgundy, Hungary, parts of Italy, and Germany. Besides all of this, he ruled the vast new domains of Columbus's discovery—half the world after the pope divided the world between Spain and Portugal.

In the Treaty of Tordesillas (1494), Pope John II divided the world—other than Europe—between Spain and Portugal. He drew a line in the Atlantic about one thousand miles west of the Cape Verde Islands. This put Brazil in Portugal's half. Spain's half began at the one-thousand-mile line. It included the rest of North and South America and all the Pacific through the Philippines. Portugal's half started at the Philippines, included Asia and Africa, plus Brazil in South America.

Charles V was busy, but he still had to respect his Uncle Frederick's demand for a trial in Germany. After all, Uncle Fred cast the deciding vote for Charles to become holy Roman emperor instead of Francis I of France. It was the only vote cast without bribery, for Fred was a simple, pious man. But the unelected Francis then allied with Turks, so Charles fought a Franco-Turkish alliance from both ends of his European empire, from Spain and from Austria.

Charles was busy, but he went to Germany to preside at Luther's trial at the Diet of Worms. Here was the most powerful man in Europe facing a mere monk. Luther was often taunted and often wondered himself. "Are you, a mere monk, the only one right and the church and ages wrong?"

Still, Luther refused to recant—unless scripture proved him wrong. Otherwise, he stood by what he believed. "*Hier stehe ich. Ich kann nicht anders. Gott helf mir.*" (Here I stand. I cannot do otherwise. God help me.) Whether he said this or not, it certainly stated his position.

Help came from Frederick who told one of his religious advisors to save Luther. "Don't tell me how, just do it." On Luther's way back to Wittenberg, he was "kidnapped" and led around in the forest until midnight then hidden in Wartburg Castle disguised as a knight. During his year of hiding, Luther translated the New Testament into German.

Other Reformers

Luther translated the New Testament into German, but less known is the fact that Melanchthon corrected the translation and corrected Luther's overemphasis on faith. In a commentary on Romans, Melanchthon affirmed faith by God's grace but also our "free will" to respond to God's grace, lest the concept become too predestined. In addition, works must flow from accepting God's grace—for the good of society.

Philipp Melanchthon (1497–1560) was the son of Georg Schwarzerd, armorer to Palatinate princes, whose capital was Heidelberg. Philipp's mother was the niece of Johann Reuchlin, a humanist and Hebrew scholar who studied in Florence. Reuchlin supervised the education of Philipp as a classic Greek scholar at Heidelberg University. In the custom of the day, Reuchlin then gave Philipp the Greek form of the family name, Melanchthon for Schwarzerd or "black earth."

Besides Greek, Philipp was a scholar of Hebrew and Hebrew scripture, as was his uncle. Such studies produced knowledgeable Christians who reemphasized the Hebrew root to Christianity, which the "disobedience" of the Jews had preserved.

Melanchthon, who was later buried in a tomb next to Luther in the church at Wittenberg, published the first systematic Reform theology and prepared the *Augsburg Confession*, which influenced other Protestant creeds. He helped set up a Protestant school system in the German principalities, whose rulers chose to become Lutheran. The Augsburg Treaty provided that "ruler decides, people abide" on whether to remain Catholic or become Lutheran. Most princes in the south were closer to Habsburg influence and remained Catholic. Northern princes chose to become Lutheran. Scandinavian kings also chose to become Lutheran.

Another Reformer was Ulrich Zwingli (1484–1531) of Zurich, Switzerland. In 1519, he preached straight through the book of Mark. A revolutionary idea! He saw scripture as a "whole" rather than lectionary pieces. He urged a return to scripture with Bible study groups. He changed the Lord's Supper into a memorial to Christ, "This do in remembrance of me." Observed on a quarterly basis, the bread and wine were passed from person to person to emphasize the idea of the priesthood of believers.

For Protestant unity in the communion service, Philip of Hesse held a conference at Marburg. Luther, Zwingli, and Martin Bucer of Strasburg were about to agree that communion was more than a remembrance. Christ was present spiritually, though not physically, as in the transubstantiation of the Catholic tradition. Melanchthon felt reunification with the Catholic Church was still possible, so Protestant unity failed when he did not agree. Melanchthon was the systematic theologian but erred at Marburg. Luther was the firebrand. He erred in his eccentric later years.

Zwingli felt God was sovereign in all aspects of life. Religion. Society. Everything fit together in a close church-state relation. Zwingli persuaded Zurich to agree to his church ruling the state. Luther, on the other hand, yielded authority to the state, to his benefactor, Frederick. Luther was unsupportive of Zwingli's involvement in the religious wars of the Swiss cantons. Five Catholic versus eight Protestant. Zwingli was killed in the wars. His untimely death was probably the reason he formed no denomination. His strict moral ideas, which were upheld in the close church-state structure he advocated, led to puritan simplicity, sometimes puritanical.

John Calvin adopted much from Zwingli. French-born, lawyer-trained, Jean Cauvin (1509–1564) absorbed Reform ideas while studying in France. He was forced to leave and ended up in Geneva, which later became a political theocracy that ordered every aspect of life. The new church structure had no bishops but rested on presbyters (elders and deacons). Thus, Presbyterians.

When in the minority, Calvinists insisted on individual rights, which they recognized in their representative church government. This provided the pattern for many secular governments. But when in control, they were often not quite so tolerant, as in Calvin's Geneva, Oliver Cromwell's England, and the Puritans in Massachusetts. For example, Servetus was allowed to be burned at the stake in Geneva because of his Unitarian heresy, which denied the Trinity and the divinity of Christ—a position that may be arguable, but not burnable.

John Knox (1505–1572) took Calvinism to Scotland, which was the only country where Presbyterianism became the national church. They tried to spread into England, but Henry VIII (1509–1547) already set the course for England.

Henry wanted to marry Anne Boleyn for a male heir. The pope refused to grant his divorce from Catherine of Aragon, who was the aunt of Holy Roman Emperor Charles V. So Henry VIII established the Church of England (the Anglican Church) with himself as head. He used disendowed lands of the Catholic Church (a third of England) to reward the nobles who supported him. (Luther wanted disendowed property used to fund education).

Henry's daughter Mary (by Catherine of Aragon) married Philip II of Spain, the son of Charles V. She took England back to Catholicism for five years before she died in 1558. Henry's daughter Elizabeth (by Anne Boleyn) succeeded Mary and ruled until 1603. Elizabeth preferred the Reformed Church of England because she had more power when she was also head of the church.

Counter-Reformation

By the time Elizabeth became queen of England, Ignatius Loyola (1491–1556) founded the Society of Jesus, the Jesuits, and started the Counter-Reformation. The three I's of the movement were: Ignatius, inquisition, and index. The Inquisition was tightened a few more turns. The index was a list of books, both bidden and forbidden, to be read. On the bidden list was Loyola's *Spiritual Exercises*, which included the following admonition:

> If she [the church] defined anything to be black which to our eyes appears to be white, we ought in like manner to pronounce it to be black.[15]

Notice the difference between this idea and that of the reformers who were trying to get each person, each individual, to think for himself.

When the Jews failed to accept Christ, God went to the Gentiles. When the Catholics failed to reform, God went to the Protestants. Rather, the thrust of spiritual evolution moved with Protestants to America, whose providential rediscovery coincided with the Reformation. Even so, Europeans fought for another century over an idea whose time had come, no matter how they tried to stop it. And the heirs of Charles V did try.

Charles V abdicated after a forty-year reign. He gave the Austrian HRE part of the empire to his brother Ferdinand I and the Spanish part to his son Philip II (as on the earlier genealogy chart). Ferd I was succeeded by Ferd II. Jesuits took the Counter-Reformation to Austria and persuaded Ferdinand II to bring Lutheran princes in Germany back into the Catholic fold. The Thirty Years' War (1618–1648) devastated Germany yet ended

---

15. Brinton, et al, *A History of Civilization* (New Jersey: Prentice Hall, 1976), 482.

with the same Augsburg conclusion: Ruler decides. People abide. Ferdinand fought for naught. The north remained Protestant but took a century to recover as Berlin and Prussia rose to unite Germany (through the Hohenzollerns of Brandenburg-Prussia).

Philip II was overburdened with the task of ruling Spain and its worldwide empire that now included Portugal's half of the world. Still he felt compelled to stamp out the Reformation in the Netherlands and England. He was sure that wherever Protestants fought, Elizabeth sent money—probably his own gold taken from his ships by Francis Drake and other privateers.

Drake was an international celebrity. This one man pitted against the greatest king in Christendom was followed in many parts of Europe by newspapers and pamphleteers. Perhaps Drake was influenced by his Puritan lay-preacher father, for he felt he upheld the Reformation just as Phillip upheld the Counter-Reformation.

Drake had thirty ships with "public" orders from Elizabeth to show *no* hostility to Spain, but with secret orders to stop Philip, who was assembling an armada to invade England in 1588. Philip wrote *nonsense* in the margin of a report that predicted an easy victory. An armada of over five hundred ships meant thirty thousand sailors and sixty thousand soldiers, plus tons of provisions.[16]

Drake stopped at the port of Sagres where Portuguese prince Henry the Navigator (1374–1460) built his complex for castle, library, astronomers, and seamen. Drake set fire to it. Then he set fire to coastal cargo boats loaded with seasoned barrel staves ready for the coopers. Tons of provisions stored in barrels made from unseasoned green staves spoiled during the expedition.[17]

---

16. Garrett Mattingly, *The Armada* (Boston: Houghton Mifflin Co., 1959), 76, 80.
17. Ibid., 115, 121.

The whole encounter was bungled on both sides but shifted in favor of England when the wind shifted, and the Spanish could not land. An accident? Or providence? England and the Netherlands remained Protestant. One of Elizabeth's armada medals read, "God breathed and they were scattered."[18]

The Netherlands immediately became an important commercial sea power with worldwide colonies. Elizabethan England gradually shifted into the commercial stage while Spain went into rapid decline. Philip thought he had a new source of income when he gained Portugal, but all he got was a "bankrupt whole sale grocery business."[19]

When Philip extended the Inquisition into Portugal, the Moors and Jews who had been expelled from Spain were then routed from Portugal. Most fled to the Netherlands. This shortsighted policy had already ruined the solid economic base that Islamic civilization had built in Spain: rich agriculture with terraces and irrigation for vineyards and crops; industries such as lens grinding, crafting of swords, and cutlery thanks to Spanish mines and eastern formulas (Damascus steel); plus commerce through Moorish trade connections with the Far East. But with the expulsion of Jews and Moors, techniques were lost, and trade connections were broken.

> The gold and silver from America staved off bankruptcy for a while, for gold gives the illusion of wealth, but provides nothing of solid value. It generates no productive work for the people, the absence of which robs them of values and positive purpose.[20]

---

18. Ibid., 390.
19. Ibid., 123.
20. Ibid., page number undetermined.

Spain became impoverished, especially after the gold went to pay for armada expenses and to build a new navy with more maneuverable English-style ships. This was the end of the galleons that were used since Roman times. Incidentally, because of confusions in his accounting of armada expenses, Cervantes was sent to prison where he wrote *Don Quixote.*

The armada fiasco assured that England and the Netherlands remained Protestant. A reformed and vigorous Christianity, which reached back through the Hebrew root of the faith to man's common origin, would now be taken to America. A new society rooted in the heritage of a reformed Judeo-Christian faith and in Western civilization would sprout with a renewed creation relation then grow through the normal social stages to ultimately produce a new-world spirit of understanding that would bring mankind closer to fulfillment.

The unity of society and unity of the church of the early Middle Ages is to be replaced with unity of the person through the spiritual integrity of each individual thinking for himself— thanks to the priesthood of the believer.

5

New-World Spirit

Climate of the Times, ca. 1500

The New World was discovered just in time to provide a refuge for Protestants so a New World Spirit might evolve and be fulfilled.

This new-world spirit, which began in the climate of the times around 1500, had three main thrusts of development represented by three men.

- Galileo, science-technology. He used the lens and was father of modern science, but he was closer to 1600.
- Columbus, social-political. He discovered America where it took place.
- Luther, ideational-spiritual-individual development. Through the Reformation's "priesthood of believer."

Finally, each individual will think for himself and understand what Jesus meant when he said that ideas and attitudes held and cherished in the heart—and mind—were more important than law, for ideas and beliefs do shape our actions and our world.

During the next five hundred years, these three thrusts of development would gradually be fulfilled so a new-world spirit might evolve as Western civilization was carried into all the world.

Western civ was first carried to the New World by the Spanish who transferred Old World social and religious ideas almost intact. New ideas came with Christianity's Protestant—and provident—shift to America after the Dutch and English defeated the Spanish Armada.

Dutch Protestants settled the Hudson Valley and New Amsterdam (New York) after Henry Hudson discovered them in 1609 and after Peter Minuit bought Manhattan Island from the Indians for twenty-eight dollars in 1626. Dutch sea power remained supreme in the world until 1664, when it was reduced by a brief English-French alliance as the English forsook their longtime ally to boost their own power on the sea and in the world. Dutch New Amsterdam was a mixed colony of Spanish, Germans, Swedes, and Norse, who did not feel enough allegiance to assist in the Dutch War. But Governor Peter Stuyvesant did negotiate a guarantee of their rights in their "Articles of Capitulation." (The articles were later echoed in the Bill of Rights that was added to the US Constitution.)[1]

England merged the Dutch colonies with its own. By then, English Protestants had settled Jamestown in 1607 and Plymouth in 1620. Maryland was settled in 1632 as a refuge for Catholics who felt the persecutions of Anglican Bishop Laud as much as the Puritans who founded Plymouth. Quaker William Penn (1682) enticed colonists with offers of free or cheap land plus political

1. Thomas Lipscomb, review of *The Island at the Center of the World*, by Russell Shorto, *The Wall Street Journal*, March 16, 2004.

and religious freedom. A century later, Philadelphia, the city of brotherly love, was a center of learning, science, arts, commerce— second to London in the British Empire—and the birthplace of American independence.

But the 1600s and early 1700s were difficult for the colonists. They scratched to survive. They literally scratched a hole for a fish and a kernel of corn. No one could rest on his title—not even the third son of a duke. All must work to survive. Finally, a few crude settlements of wattle-and-daub houses with stockade fences were built—in a repeat of Europe at the beginning of the Dark Ages.

The English colonists started anew at the agrarian stage with a down-to-earth grasp of reality and with a closeness to nature—to creation and the Creator—which civilization seems to destroy. Americans struggled with survival while Europeans moved into the Enlightenment.

Incidentally, Czar Peter toured Europe in the early 1700s and took the Enlightenment back to Russia, but without the Reformation. He cut off the beards of the patriarchs, but that was not exactly in-depth reform. So Russia was shortchanged again as it was when Czar Ivan took dying Byzantine civ to Moscow after the fall of Constantinople.

Enlightenment

The Enlightenment was an age of reason and science. It started with the lens of the telescope and microscope, plus other inventions, including the mathematics of calculus, analytic geometry, etc. The "new" scientific method of empirical reasoning from actual experience and observation (as in the Old Testament) was augmented with experiments for proof rather than merely using abstract logic. A big influence was the new think-for-yourself idea embodied in the Reformation. As Luther stood by his convictions, now Galileo, even while recanting, asserted, "Nevertheless, it so moves"—the earth around the sun.

With these inventions and this kind of thinking, man sought to learn the laws of nature. Western civ was at the point where man's underlying belief in God's orderly creation made the search for uniform laws logical. A belief in chance would never have made the search for laws logical. Yet as man searched, he could step aside, separated from creation, and view it objectively.

Thus, modern science rested primarily on three factors that prevailed in the climate of the times at 1500.

1. The inventions of math and instruments
2. The scientific method of thought from experience and for oneself
3. A detached but underlying belief in God's orderly universe

Galileo, Kepler, Copernicus studied the heavens; Newton, gravity; Lavoisier, chemistry; Franklin, electricity. Linnaeus saw order in the plants and animals he classified.[2] French encyclopedists gathered knowledge so people could be instructed in natural laws and science. Enlightened with sci-tech knowledge, superstition was to be exposed and nature controlled.

But "human" nature was not to be controlled, for man was by nature "good;" and through science and reason, he would create a better world all *by himself.* The romantic fallacy of man's innate goodness is quite different from the biblical concept that humans do err and miss the mark—even sin.

---

2. Galilei Galileo (1564–1642) was Italian; Johannes Kepler (1571–1630), German; Nicolaus Copernicus (1473–1543), Polish; Isaac Newton (1642–1727), English; Antoine Lavoisier (1743–1794), French; Benjamin Franklin (1706-1790), American; Carolus Linnaeus (1707–1778); Swedish.

Enlightened man had great faith in his natural goodness and his reason, plus the knowledge *he* discovered—as if God had nothing to do with it. Yet when God wants something known in the world, He prepares the spirit of the times, the zeitgeist, so that His revelation will be discovered. There is always someone who will pick the apple from the tree, watch it fall to earth, or take a few more bites to get to the core of knowledge. We now have many bites (even bytes) of knowledge but still no core, for knowledge became more and more fragmented as it became more separated and more specialized.

Social-Political Contracts

The natural and social sciences parted company. John Locke contributed to the separation with his treatises on government. Man submits to government because it is convenient to do so; otherwise, man is "by nature free, equal and independent."[3] Locke seemed to believe that man is by nature free, yet man is free of nature. Locke discounted heredity while he counted environment and experience for everything in man's development.[4]

The idea arose that with the "right kind of chalk to use on the blank slates of impressionable young minds," teachers could remold rising generations.[5]

---

3. Brinton, et al, *History of Civilization*, vol. 2, 50.
4. How ironic. Heredity was discounted when nature was so important. Not only heredity and environment, but *will* must also be seen as a factor in each life. Adding will could change our concepts of education, sociology, psychology, and religion.
5. R. L. Bruckberger, *Image of America* (New York: The Viking Press, 1959). In the 1950s this French Catholic priest saw the importance of the reformed Judeo-Christian tradition in the founding of the United States as he compared the American Revolution to the French Revolution.

Oblivious to the incongruities of Enlightenment thinking—control nature but not human nature—Rousseau found the chalk used by generations of teachers to write on the blank slates of young minds. Since nature dignifies while civilization corrupts, Rousseau proposed a natural education in his novel *Emile*. The enlightened tutor let his pupil learn from nature while they roamed the woods as Emile's innate "good" nature was inclined. An indulged student with a one-on-one tutor! What a formula for mass education. Nevertheless, through *Emile*, Rousseau became the father of modern education, which has not yet abandoned him, even though he abandoned his own four children to foundling homes.

Rousseau was also the father of the French Revolution through his book *Social Contract*. Although civilization corrupts, it cannot be abandoned (no foundling homes), so a social contract must be made between people and government. Also, a "civil religion" must be instituted so the state no longer has to compete with the church for the allegiance of the people. Incredible! Civilization corrupts, so make it a religion? Worship the state?

In the meantime, English colonists were on their way to a different kind of social contract. In America, they found a frontier where they could make a fresh start with a new slate for the society they founded. Although Europe's slate was far from blank, visionaries would erase the slate and wipe it clean in order to start over. The erased slate, *tabula rasa*, was an important but mistaken notion adopted by the French and later by Marxist revolutionaries.

Actually, the way to evolve is to build on what went before. The underlying pattern of evolution is *cumulative* development, which builds on what went before. "The great, successful revolutions preserved, transformed, created even more than they destroyed."[6] This is what the Americans did in their revolution.

---

6.   Ibid, 63

American Declaration of Independence

Why did Americans revolt? Britain had ruled the colonies with benign neglect during the British Civil War and Cromwell period, ca. 1650, when the colonies were established. Benign neglect continued through most of the next century while England acquired its worldwide empire beginning with the Dutch colonies in 1664. By then, England had given up on conquests in Europe.

England then fought colonial wars while various allies in Europe fought the continental part of the war. These were mostly wars of succession in Spain, Austria, and Poland. All had different names in America. The War of Spanish Succession was Queen Anne's War (1701–1714), after which Britain got Gibraltar from Spain and all of French Canada except Quebec. The War of Austrian Succession (1740–1748) was King George's War in America (George II). Marie Therese retained her HRE throne, but since England allied with losing Austria, it gained nothing. Frederick II of Prussia-Germany won the war and gained enough territory and prestige to enhance his title to Frederick the Great.

England decided to fight with the winning Frederick in the Seven Years' War (1756–1763). While Prussia fought the continental war against France, England fought in India and America. Called the French and Indian War in America, soldiers such as George Washington fought for England and gained experience they later used in the revolution. This war was the most devastating in French history. The Treaty of Paris (1763) ousted France from India and from Quebec.

Benign neglect was over. England began a century of economic leadership (1770–1870) by enforcing restrictive mercantile laws in its worldwide colonies and collecting taxes. The colonists were not allowed to manufacture but had to buy from or through the British. (This was harder on India, which already had a manufacturing economy with textile production that was now dismantled.) In America, the Hat Act forbade the export of hats. The Iron Act restricted the erection of manufacturing plants. Many items were taxed. Stamps on documents. The tax on tea led to the Boston Tea Party.

After the "party" was over, George III decreed Boston Harbor closed. He announced,

"The die is cast. The Colonies must either triumph or submit."

When the British came to close the harbor, General Gage sent one thousand men to destroy the colonial supply depot in Concord. On their way to Concord, the British skirmished with minutemen militia but destroyed the depot. On their way back from Concord, they met the whole countryside up in arms.

Many years later, a veteran of Concord was interviewed:[7]

> "Why did you fight? Because of intolerable oppression?"
>
> "Did not feel any."
>
> "Stamp Act?"
>
> "Never saw one stamp."
>
> "Tea Tax?"
>
> "Never drank it."
>
> "From reading Locke, etc., on principles of liberty?"
>
> "Read only the Bible, Catechism, Watts' Psalms and Hymns, and the Almanack."
>
> "Then why?"
>
> "What we meant in going for those red coats was this: we always governed ourselves and we always meant to. They didn't mean we should."

After the skirmish at Concord, the First Continental Congress sent a declaration of resolves to George III:

---

7. R. L. Bruckberger, *Image of America* (New York: The Viking Press, 1959), 41.

> By the laws of nature, [by] the English constitution and [by] their charters they had the right to *life, liberty and property*, which they did not lose by emigrating to America...since the colonists were not represented in the British Parliament, taxation and internal policy should be decided in their own legislatures...subject to the King's veto.

But why should parliament let the colonists rule themselves when it knew better? The English thought Americans were socially inferior, "scum and off-scouring of all nations," while the Americans thought the English were as "corrupt as Babylon."[8]

George III decreed the colonies outside the protection of the empire and its fleet. The colonies sought alliance with France. This was an act of treason since they were not a sovereign nation. King Louis XVI insisted the Americans declare their independence. Then France was ready to help and to recoup its losses of 1763.

The men who drafted the Declaration of Independence were far better than the philosophy of their day because their thinking was the product of their character as Americans. Many were touched by the Enlightenment as Jefferson, who once asked, "Why should I go in search of Moses to find out what God said to Jean-Jacques Rousseau?"[9]

Fortunately, the Enlightenment group was balanced by the contingent from New England, which was still as close to Moses as the old Concord veteran and expressed the general feeling of the American people.

Thomas Jefferson wrote the declaration because he had a "peculiar felicity of expression," but the New England contingent inserted the phrases that refer to Creator, providence, and Judge:

---

8. Ibid., 35.
9. Ibid., 90.

> When in the course of human events…people dissolve political bonds…a decent respect [for] mankind requires they declare the causes…We hold these truths to be self-evident, that all men are created equal, that they are endowed by their *Creator* with certain inalienable rights… life, liberty and the *pursuit of happiness*.[10]

Thus they declared their rights then applied them to the American situation and concluded,

> We…representatives…appealing to the *Supreme Judge* of the world for rectitude of our intentions, do…declare, that these United Colonies are…Free and Independent States…And…with a firm reliance on the protection of *divine Providence*, we mutually pledge to each other our Lives, our Fortunes, and our sacred Honor.

Through their recognition of God as Creator, Providence, and Judge, the Americans abolished divine right in politics. On the other hand, the French extended divine right when they proclaimed that "the origin of all sovereignty resides essentially in the nation." Any dictator would agree to that.

Father Bruckberger explained,[11]

---

10. Note the change from "life, liberty and *property*" in the resolves to "life, liberty and *pursuit of happiness*." Property provides the security that assures life and liberty. The pursuit of happiness assures neither but has become the number-one pursuit in twentieth-century America and has produced unbelievably ridiculous but serious results. On the other hand, "property" teaches responsibility for the maintenance and stewardship of one's surroundings and one's environment. How many people came to United States for happiness? How many for economic reasons? For property?

11. Ibid., 100–104.

America abolished divine right in politics [not merely the divine right of kings]—and this is where Congress was right and Jefferson was wrong—it is not enough merely to give the people full sovereignty. It must also be recognized that men's inalienable rights, upon which their sovereignty is based, *derive from God, Creator, Providence and Judge.* It is true that people have rights…but not every right is theirs. They have no right to deify themselves. Since their rights derive from God, they can exercise them only according to God's will. In their very sovereignty the people are subject to God. Without religion even democracy is exposed to all the perils of tyranny.

This is where we have gone astray. We try to export freedom and democracy without our reformed Judeo-Christian base. Yet the Reformation provided the underlying idea, "If you can think for yourself in religious matters, why not also in political?" The government cannot stress our reformed Judeo-Christian base because we have separation of church and state. And that is good. But the church should certainly be able to acknowledge this and teach it to our youth before they leave home and go out into the world.

People say, "I'll take the rights, but not God, thank you. And not the responsibility"; however,

The Declaration places squarely on the shoulders of the individual the full responsibility, the full burden of his destiny, and not only his own personal destiny, but of his *common destiny*, with all other men in its ultimate fulfillment.[12]

---

12. Ibid., 107. Julian Hartt in *Lost Image of God* Man (LSU Press, p.100) also saw the link between freedom and responsibility. 'Freedom is a dreadful burden, if it means that a man is absolutely responsible for himself and can really and finally be only what he is prepared to resolve to become.'

Father Bruckberger felt the declaration was providentially inspired:[13]

> It is absolutely astounding that the 18th century produced such a document. It is like a proof of the ceaseless workings of God's Providence. Just as it stands this Declaration is so complete, so perfect, that it has the quality of a natural revelation, almost indeed as though a Divine grace had been conferred upon the American nation...What age before the 18th century could have produced this Declaration?

And what age since?

The Revolution

The Declaration of Independence was followed by war. Most of Europe joined the fray, as they had for centuries, to "balance" power in Europe. They also wanted to recoup losses to England. France wanted India and Quebec. Spain wanted Gibraltar and Jamaica.

France declared war and sent troops and ships. Spain remained neutral (for most of the war) but assisted from Florida and New Orleans. American ships fleeing the British were given safe harbor in New Orleans. Spain sent cattle drives from Texas and helped Americans bypass the eastern blockade by allowing supplies to go through New Orleans and up the Mississippi.

Finally in 1781, after five cruel years of war, George Washington defeated Charles Cornwallis at Yorktown, Virginia, with help from Marquis de Lafayette and the French navy. England wanted peace with the colonists before other nations came to the peace table to claim their piece of the world. The loss of thirteen colonies was small compared to French and Spanish

---

13. Ibid., 99.

demands. After all, the colonies could be reclaimed. The final formal peace with France and Spain and the new United States of America was made two years later. However, the War of 1812 was needed to reaffirm American independence.

France was the big loser in the American Revolution. They regained no territory, but their debt doubled and redoubled so quickly that the French Revolution became inevitable. The Third Estate (the people) needed tax relief, but the First and Second Estate (clergy and nobility) would not give up their largely exempt tax status. Even though they did not fulfill the obligations of their class, they claimed all the privileges. Thomas Jefferson suggested a limited constitutional monarchy.

The Jacobins were obsessed with a clean slate and guillotined the nobility to erase the slate.

> A nation can regenerate itself only upon mounds of corpses...What makes a Republic is the total destruction of whatever stands in its way....A government has for principles either virtue or terror.[14]

The Jacobin reign of terror was superbly organized from commune to assembly,[15] but it was such a caricature of government à la Rousseau that Napoleon soon followed.

Napoleon swept through Europe until his Grande Armée was turned back from Moscow in ice and snow. He met defeat at Leipzig, then again at Waterloo.

Napoleon changed Europe, yet it remained the same. He broke the church monopoly on education in France and reduced the political power of the Vatican. He also broke the official power

---

14. Ibid., 64–65
15. The terror was later repeated in Soviet terror from commune to Comintern (Communist International). Charles Dickens's *A Tale of Two Cities* introduced many young people to the French Revolution.

of the nobility, but the prestige of class continued in Europe. Although Napoleon reduced the power of the nobility, he divorced Josephine in order to marry an Austrian HRE Habsburg.

The peace treaty after Waterloo reinstated the monarchies under constitutions. Barely were the crowns in place than the constitutions were shredded by kings, who wanted absolute power, or by radicals, who demanded republics without monarchs. Moderates seldom won.

During uprisings in capitals of Europe between 1820–1830, many nations won their independence. Mexico gained independence in 1821, three hundred years after Cortez conquered the Aztec in 1521. Other South American countries also became independent of Spain.

Physical-Economic Freedom

The climate of the times after the Reformation set in motion three thrusts of development represented by three men, as mentioned before.

1. Galileo, science-technology, for he used the lens and was the father of modern science.
2. Columbus, social-political, for he discovered America where it took place.
3. Luther, ideational-spiritual-individual, for with the Reformation's "priesthood of believer," each individual is to think for himself.

The thrust to social-political freedom moved forward with the American Declaration of Independence while science-technology worked to bring physical freedom to mankind through labor-saving devices. But workers have not always received the benefits because of economic ideas. In the Middle Ages, people suffered from strange "theo-economic" ideas that condemned commerce and damned banking. Also, taxes were exempted or assessed based on "estates" or classes. Even though classes were obsolete ever since the Reformation recognized the individual, Europeans did not seem to understand. They still sought class solutions, especially after economics was "discovered."

Yet all civilizations, since earliest Sumerian, have risen through three main economic stages: from agri-craft, through different levels of industrial-commercial, to the financial stage. More specifically, after the agrarian-craft stage comes simple manufacture and trade with limited literacy (what we call pre-civ, third-world, or underdeveloped.) This advances to more complex industrial-commercial economies. Banking, insurance, and a stock market emerge to facilitate the commerce. More wealth provides funds for a literate culture and the flowering of civilization. But at the present time, the financial-intellectual sector dominates so much of the economy that it is a bit tilted and off base.

Nations thrived on a balanced economy until the agrarian root—with a natural closeness to creation and the Creator—was neglected, but the obsolescence of classes and importance of the agrarian root were both ignored as Europe moved into the financial stage with *Euro-style capitalism.*

As economics became part of social science, humanistic materialism was born to play a major role in the next centuries. First, the classic humanism of Greece and Rome evolved into Christian humanism through humanists such as Erasmus during the Reformation. Then, as the influence of the church ebbed, the Christian part was deleted, and the economics of materialism was added. Thus *humanistic materialism* evolved.

Christianity, which was so dynamic during the Reformation, was less so after the Enlightenment as it began to adopt from secular thought, from what was fashionable. This is why secular ideas, such as economics, must be examined.

In the eighteenth century, Adam Smith (1723–1790) "discovered" economics. Since his *Wealth of Nations* was written in a country with a naturally balanced economy, he saw "general plenty" diffused through "natural laws" of supply and demand.

In the nineteenth century, England moved into the financial stage with a shift in population from rural to urban on an overpopulated island. So up popped the cheap-bread issue and up popped Thomas Malthus (1766–1834), who thought population had to be controlled lest it outstrips production and people merely breed more vice and corruption. (For centuries, Europe eased its overpopulation through emigration to America.)

David Ricardo (1776–1823) saw economics from a global viewpoint. This justified mercantilism, with the importation of cheap bread and raw materials from countries regarded as colonials.

Harrison Brown analyzed nineteenth-century England:[16]

> The island civilization succumbed to the temptations that had faced the Greeks and Romans before them. Food could be obtained less expensively outside the island, notably from America...Local agriculture declined...and the people...became largely dependent upon food imports for their survival...The overthrow of the British landed aristocracy by the far distant democracy of American farmers was one outcome of this change. An even more important consequence has been the general divorce of Englishmen from life in contact with nature, which in all previous ages had helped to form the mind and the imagination of the island race.

England abandoned its agrarian base. Competition cut its industrial-commercial lead. England became the financial center

---

16. G. M. Trevelyan, *English Social History*, cited in Harrison Brown, *Challenge of Man's Future* (New York: Viking Press, 1954), 39.

of the world during the nineteenth century but lost its balanced economy. Money supply and social-economic theories emerged to solve the urban squalor and overpopulation of the cities. Charles Dickens (1812–1870) described this "Dickensian" world.

John Stuart Mill (1806–1848) advocated public employment programs and ownership of factories by workers with wages according to merit.

Robert Owens (1776–1848) proposed "company stores" that he set up in England and "Utopian communes" that he set up in America. He rose through the ranks of industry yet failed to recognize practical reality. He thought environment caused the evils of workers, such as drunkenness and illicit sex, so he provided company houses, a company store, and a company bank. But he still paid low wages.

In contrast to this, Henry Ford started American-style capitalism. Ford was a product of the Midwest frontier where people still respected one another as equals. Bruckberger called him a "messiah of the machine" because Ford wanted to lift drudgery from the backs of men and put it onto steel and machines in factories, agriculture, and transportation. Therefore, his Model T. When it finally started rolling off the assembly line, Ford met with his board of directors. At that time, wages were $2.50 for an entire nine-hour day. (Ford historians recorded the event of January 1, 1914.)

> Ford covered his blackboard with figures. When he set down the total for wages, they seemed too small compared with the anticipated profits. He kept raising the wages... to $3.00, to $3.50, then over protests...to $4.00 and $4.50. "Well," one man snapped, "It's up to $4.75. I dare you to make it $5.00"...And he did.

A few days later, the company announced an eight-hour, five-dollar day. Ford commented, "This is neither charity nor wages, but profit sharing and efficiency engineering." "When you pay men well, you can talk to them." "If you cut wages, you just cut the number of your own customers."

Ford's workers could live where they wanted and buy what they wanted, even his Model T, if he kept reducing the price so they could afford it.

This illustrates the difference between European- and American-style capitalism, between the European class attitude of ingrained patronage—with *noblesse oblige* perhaps but still with a condescending handed-down-from-above attitude *von oben herab*—and the American attitude of respect for one's fellow man as an equal, which was relearned on each new frontier.

Henry Ford was a product of the Midwest frontier of the nineteenth century, even though his ideas belong to the twentieth when his brand of American capitalism became the norm. Until then, American "robber barons" adopted Euro-style capitalism.

It was Euro-style capitalism that Marx rebelled against. Karl Marx (1818–1883) rebelled against his family, his religion, and his nation (Judaism and Germany). Then he took refuge in England and took support from Friedrich Engels while he fashioned a system that extolled freedom but enslaved people as never before.

Marx applied Hegel's dialectic principle of "thesis-antithesis-synthesis" to history and economic materialism. His "dialectic materialism" would play a large role in the twentieth century as dialectic and humanistic materialism clashed. Therefore, some understanding is necessary. In dialectic materialism, the evils of the past, namely Euro-style capitalism (thesis), must be swept away by revolution for a clean slate (antithesis) as history inevitably turned to his kind of materialism (synthesis). He saw two great forces at work in society and history toward this end: 1) the struggle of man against nature and 2) the struggle of man against man.

Marx traced the man-against-man struggle from exploitation in the patriarchal family through slave-based economies to feudal serfdom and finally the wage system of capitalism, which was economic slavery. Marx figured that production was sufficient to provide plenty for all if capitalists did not prevent modern technology (exactly the opposite happened) and if production was redistributed "*from* each according to ability and *to* each according to need."

Marx and his family had needs that he failed to supply, so his theory justified the aid he received from the textile wealth of capitalist Engels. Yet bourgeois owners such as his patron-friend were to be overthrown by the proletariat working class who would form a government that owned all the divested property (there went his support from Engels). Equitable distribution was to be made according to need, but who can imagine a government benevolent enough to underwrite the needs of someone sitting in a library plotting its overthrow? England's did. The United States' might. Marx's never.

The great watershed date of Euro history was to be 1848, the year of *The Communist Manifesto* and workers' revolution, which assured workers they had "nothing to lose but their chains." The revolution failed in 1848 but succeeded in 1917 in Russia. Lenin chose Marxism, which he instituted with the terror of Jacobin-type organization from commune to Comintern (Communist International).

Poor Russia was shortchanged again—by a theory that was misconceived because the class system was already obsolete—and by then (since 1914), Henry Ford had emancipated workers by shifting slavery to machines and by doubling wages to five dollars a day for a shorter eight-hour day. Thus, Ford helped abolish both physical and economic slavery.

Thanks to machines, ours is the first time in history that civilization can exist without a slave base. Modern science-technology, which has evolved since Galileo, has finally freed man from physical and economic bondage.

Through Columbus's discovery of America, the United States was founded and found the way to freedom from social-political bondage, as expressed in the Declaration of Independence. But this is not yet fully understood, for we fail to acknowledge the Judeo-Christian base. Or that human rights derive from God, Creator-Providence-Judge. Or that rights entail responsibility.

In America, the idea whose time had come with Luther and the Reformation, the idea of the person as an individual free to think for himself and free from conceptual bondage, would struggle to become real in the twentieth century.

6

Twentieth-Century Chaos

Europe's Peak

At the turn of the twentieth century, Western civilization in Europe was at its peak. The peak that precedes the fall.

> By 1914 Europe stood in a relation to the rest of mankind never before achieved by any other civilization. She was the hub of the world...Her unparalleled position was not alone the result of imperialism and capitalistic enterprise, it was based on cultural foundations truly unique in the history of mankind...Few Europeans seem to have been apprehensive either of war or of defeat. It was a general assumption that the privileged position of the European countries would be maintained *ad infinitum*...though frail and precarious was their position.'[1]

---

1.   Gerhard Masur, *Prophets of Yesterday: Studies in European Culture, 1890–1914* (London: Macmillan, 1961), 3, 6. When I read Masur, I realized

To be fair, not too much was known about previous civilizations except the Greek and Roman. The Rosetta Stone, which Napoleon brought back from Egypt, was not deciphered until mid-nineteenth century, and our most important archeological discoveries came after mid-twentieth. Only now can we appreciate the way the Hebrews reached back in a direct line to the dawn of history. No wonder Europeans at the turn of the century thought nothing like Western civilization had happened to the world before and all should be glad to drink at the fount of Western culture.

Nevertheless, "the cavalier manner in which Europe thought they could divide up the world was unbelievable."[2] Ever since the papal decree of 1494, which divided the whole world (other than Europe) between Spain and Portugal, European nations took what and as they pleased, answerable only to one another—until World War I.

World War I was a fitting finale as Europeans played their age-old war game of noble vengeance, political put-down, balance of power, and heroic glory. The war began because insufficient apologies were offered when the Habsburg heir to the Austrian throne, Francis Ferdinand, was assassinated in Serbia. So "Princip's revolver was eventually to kill some 10 million men."[3] Millions more died of starvation and the 1918 flu.

Everyone thought the war would follow the age-old format with uniformed soldiers facing one another while cavalry horses pranced around them. But new dimensions of gore were added— tanks, trenches, barbed wire, poison gas, U-boats, airplanes.

---

why my grandfather thought like he did. Friedrich Schlennstedt grew to maturity in 1890s Berlin. We absorbed his European viewpoint even in the hinterlands of Texas.

2. Brinton, et al, *History of Civilization*, vol. 2, 344.

3. Ibid., 375.

When the cream of European manhood was slaughtered, there was precious little glory.

Yet for nearly three years, British and French troops sat in trenches facing German trenches on the other side of no-man's-land. They even reached a point of relative ease in their dirt trenches protected behind barbed-wire entanglements. When General John Pershing came with his American Expeditionary Forces, he was expected to place his troops under the French and British stalemate.

General Pershing came to fight and win the war, so he demanded that *he* lead the American forces. He sat for six weeks, encamped with his troops, until he was given command. He then ordered rolls and rolls of chicken wire. He also ordered that it take priority over pool tables being sent from England. When the chicken wire finally arrived, Pershing simply unrolled it over the barbed-wire barriers. The AEF went over the top and took the Germans by surprise. The American forces moved so fast they had to keep telling the French to lift their artillery above the advancing Americans. They pushed on to victory at Saint-Mihiel and the Argonne. Within months, armistice was declared—on the eleventh hour of the eleventh day of the eleventh month of 1918.[4]

Americans went "over there" to fight and win for principles—and propaganda—as new heroics were substituted for old, but slogans cannot be spread without someone believing them. Americans believed. They fought and won the "war to end all wars" and "to make the world safe for democracy."

Imperialism was over. Four empires ended abruptly with the war: the Austrian, German, Russian, and Turkish Ottoman.

---

4. The source for most information on World War I was my father, Hugo Bachle. He was with AEF for the entire expedition. When they were fighting the war to end all wars, he never thought he would have a son who had to go to war.

Slowly, two more would crumble, the French and the British. The United States was also obliged to abandon its policy of Manifest Destiny.[5]

As Europeans fell from the heights of 1900, their naive superiority was shattered. Many sensed the end of their civilization, but the dynamic thrust of Western civilization had already shifted to the United States.

Turn-of-the-Century Prophets

Even though the dynamic force of Western civ had shifted to the New World, America remained an intellectual colony of Europe for most of the century.

Turn-of-the-century Euro prophets shaped the twentieth century as their ideas were slowly adopted. The first to adopt the ideas were *avant-garde* intellectuals and artists in the 1920s. Acceptance was delayed in 1930s and 1940s by the stark reality of the Depression and World War II. Dissemination reached the masses during the 1960s and 1970s.

Since the Euro prophets set in motion the currents of thought that left our civilization adrift in a sea of conceptual chaos, a few of their ideas will be quickly skimmed as we search for a compass to orient ourselves.

---

5. The policy of Manifest Destiny guided the expansion of the United States across the continent. Besides the purchase of Louisiana in 1803 and Alaska in 1860s, Manifest Destiny "justified" the Mexican War of 1845 after the Republic of Texas entered the union. The United States secured the Texas border at the Rio Grande and gained the southwest territories of New Mexico, Arizona, and California from Mexico. Manifest Destiny lasted through the Spanish-American War of 1898, which transferred Puerto Rico, Hawaii, Guam, and the Philippines from Spain to the United States. After World War II, the United States granted independence to the Philippines.

Ever since the Enlightenment, knowledge became more and more fragmented and specialized. Disciplines splintered after the natural and social sciences separated and after new sciences and theories evolved. Microbiology from the work of Louis Pasteur, evolution from Charles Darwin and Alfred Russell Wallace, the physics of Michael Faraday, Max Planck, Albert Einstein, and others opened a world that was no longer a static clockwork mechanism but a constant flux between energy and matter. Yet man was still doing battle against nature. He sought to use science to harness and control nature for the sake of humanity, for humanity was securely back at the center of the universe. The battle of man versus creation would continue for most of the century.

Sigmund Freud (in his book *Civilization and its Discontents*, p. 24) advocated "going over to the attack against nature and subjecting her to the human will." But why attack nature if it was civilization that instituted the prohibitions on man that thwarted his natural instincts?

Freud identified three main instincts: 1) aggressive, 2) erotic, and 3) egoistic. The thwarting of these instincts caused the neuroses that Freud then treated with his new science, psychology. Actually, Freud's classifications were *ab*normal extremes of basic normal instincts.

1. Physical self-preservation, which must be strong for survival.
2. Social contact and companionship, which does become erotic when the companionship is missing.
3. Individual psyche-spiritual affirmation, which does become narcissistic and egoistic when the spiritual is not affirmed, when the soul or spirit is left out of psychology—when one does not look beyond self to God.

To escape civilization, some Europeans tried a return to nature, even primitive nature. Paul Gauguin went to the South Seas and painted a primitive paradise, but he failed to depict the disease, fungus, insects, and poverty suffered there.

Other Europeans took for granted the comforts of civilization against which they rebelled. Bourgeois sons, who grew up in "patrician homes" provided by their fathers and grandfathers, complained that their ancestors "left us, the later born, but two things: pretty furniture and hyper-sensitive nerves," according to Hugo von Hofmannsthal of Vienna.

René Descartes (1596–1650) originated "I think, therefore I am." With Rousseau, this became "I feel, therefore I am," and now it reached its logical conclusion with those "overdelicate nerves."

Oscar Wilde explained the position of this sensitive generation of artists:

> Too cultural and too critical, too intellectually subtle and too curious of exquisite pleasures to accept any speculations about life in exchange for life itself…meta-physics does not satisfy…it is enough that our fathers believed. They… *exhausted the faith-faculty of the species.* Their legacy to us is the skepticism of which they were afraid.[6]

In the end, Wilde gave himself over to flagrancy and "Reading Gaol."

Maurice Barrès of Lorraine described the intellectual position of the artist of the 1890s as the cult of the self, *Le Culte du moi.* (Remember Miss Piggy's "Moi" in the "Me" decades of 1970–80s.) Barrès reasoned, "But the self cannot live forever by feeding on the 'I' and is at length overtaken by the horror vacui." Barrès refused the stagnation of narcissistic emotionalism. He recognized that individuals are but fragments of a greater system of society, so he took refuge in the community (society, humanity) as a measure of mental hygiene.[7]

---

6. Masur, *Prophets of Yesterday*, 106–107.
7. Ibid., 142–143.

Man was still confused in his understanding of the individual in society. He made it an either-or situation; that is, an individual-versus-society situation rather than a harmonious interrelation. After the Reformation, the medieval idea of the unity of society was to become the unity of the person, the individual, within the whole of society. But the idea has gone off on a few tangents and taken a long time to evolve.

In fact, Lutheran theologian Jaroslav Pelikan in the 1970s said the two biggest problems facing the church were the dichotomy of the individual in society and of society in creation. This goes back to Adam and the disharmony that arose when man separated from God. In the first chapters of Genesis, man became conscious of himself as separate from God, separate from creation, and separate from society.

Every civilization and every person is a microcosm of mankind and repeats these separations. Western civilization reached the point of all three separations at the time of the Reformation. The trick is to be separate yet one as Christ showed the way—in fact, was the way—to be one with the Father, and thereby, also to be one with society and one with creation. Each person needs the paradoxical unity of this oneness in the separation of his individuality, his *self*.

As Western man became conscious of self, he became very subjective. The idea that "Nothing exists except what I experience"—existentialism—probably derived from Arthur Schopenhauer (died in 1860) and his book *The World as Will and Idea*. According to him, "the world is my idea," for man alone can think about it consciously.

Soren Kierkegaard subscribed to existentialism because it is through experience that one arrives at "truth." For him, the only truth was God, to put God first, as he explained that Abraham did when he was asked to sacrifice Isaac. Kierkegaard chose the spiritual for himself but felt that others might choose an ethical or esthetic lifestyle with equal validity. In this, he reflected his times when people, at least the intelligentsia, felt that a life dedicated to art (esthetics) or to humanity (society, his ethics) was a complete existence.

Masur summarized the "self-enchanted" esthetic movement that rose from "disenchantment" over the failure of reason and science to save the world as the Enlightenment thought it should.

> Religion, under the impact of the natural sciences, had lost the power to save men; science refused to do so. The artist, therefore proffered his solution; man should be saved through the arts…Art for art's sake began to signify art for the artist's sake…twofold isolation. He (the artist) had rejected the outside world and his portentous ego was obliged to reject all other egos…so had to depend on his own emotion…which explains why so great an emphasis was placed on Eros (to) assuage the thirst for companionship. This attitude marks the last phase of the romantic movement with its exaggerated appeal to emotion divorced from reason.
>
> From the sociological point of view, the esthetic movement was a bourgeois movement (though anti-bourgeois in tone) because its representatives, without exception, came from the middle class. None knew the struggle of the working class from direct experience… Those who awoke to it later did so through intellectual channels. Estheticism would have been impossible elsewhere: in a theocratic society it would be condemned as heresy, in aristocratic society the 'clerc' was kept in his place; nor tolerated in communistic society.[8]

The revolt of individuals against their middle-class background was uncanny in the 1900s and in the 1960s during mass

---

8. Ibid., 157.

acceptance of the idea. Perhaps the key phrase is "none knew the struggle of the working class from direct experience." Because of widespread affluence during the 1950s and 1960s and because of Pollyanna methods of teaching, which shielded children from reality or failure, few middle-class children in America knew the struggle for survival the way children of the 1930s did. The '30s children were then the youth of the '40s war years for a double dose of reality.

We might note the compensating Cinderella-type movies of the 1930s during the years of stark reality compared to the pseudorealism of movies in the 1960s and 1970s. In the latter decades, drugs were also used for expanded "reality," and natural lifestyles were assumed. But both were cop-outs rather than facing reality and coming to grips with it.

"Will" Discovered

Young people do need to come to grips with survival for a down-to-earth grasp of reality. William James saw this in a "war experience." With his idea of a war experience, plus pragmatism and creative truth, James was America's contribution to the turn-of-the-century era. James advocated "do-it-yourself" truth in his book *Will to Believe.*

> Reality is what works for us human beings...nothing fixed and certain. No absolute...Truth is what we want to believe, limited by pragmatism, by what is practical, by what works.[9]

In the 1990s, crucial segments of society subscribed to such "creative" truth. By then, Dietrich Bonhoeffer had urged real

---

9.   Brinton,et al, *History of Civilization*, vol. 2, 336.

truth (from a prison in Nazi Germany during World War II). He explained,

> Telling the truth is not solely a matter of moral character; it is also a matter of correct appreciation of real situations'... Telling the truth' must be learned...the ethical cannot be detached from reality, and consequently continual progress in learning to appreciate reality is a necessary ingredient of ethical action.

Julian Hartt, in his book *The Lost Image of Man*, also about midcentury, observed,

> Man is a singular creature...he can tell persuasive lies to himself and live with and love even the most violently distorted images of himself as if they were perfect expressions of truth.

Neither Bonhoeffer nor Hartt had the impact of the earlier "will" philosophers, whose influence continued throughout the twentieth century.

Friedrich Wilhelm Nietzsche (1844–1900), in his book *Will to Power*, advocated using will in order to become superhuman man. Hitler took this idea to disastrous conclusions because he ignored Nietzsche's other conclusion.

Although Nietzsche was one of the first "God is dead" prophets, when he extrapolated his atheism, he realized the bestial lot man would become if atheism such as his were to become widely held. He felt that morality must be instituted *as if* God exists, for if the theological foundations are destroyed, the ethical house will collapse—as it did by the end of the twentieth century.

These men were beginning to see that will must be factored into existence. *Environment* is not the only determining factor in our lives, as was thought since the beginning of the Enlightenment. *Heredity* must not be forgotten, especially now after the discovery of DNA. And *will* must be added. Actually, will is most important—each individual's will in harmony with God's will with an indwelling of God's Holy Spirit. This merging of wills is the strongest force in a person's life because only then does a person have the integrity and strength to stand up for what is right in God's eyes. As Bonhoeffer did. As Luther did. As Paul did. As even Jesus did, when he prayed in the Garden of Gethsemane: "Not my will, but Thy will be done."

A world filled with such spiritual individuals remains the unfulfilled promise of the Reformation because the churches have neglected the individual in their emphasis on social action. "Why save individuals one by one when society is damning them by the thousands?"

Carl Jung presented the other side of the argument in *The Undiscovered Self* (p. 68, 70, 75, 60, 84):

> People go on blithely organizing and believing in the sovereign remedy of mass action...Curiously enough, the churches too want to avail themselves of mass action in order to cast out the devil...the very churches whose care is the salvation of the individual soul...the individual becomes morally and spiritually inferior in the mass...if the individual is not truly regenerated in spirit, society cannot be either, for society is the sum total of individuals in need of redemption...inner man remains unchanged no matter how much community he has. Environment cannot give what comes only with effort....a deep-seated change of inner man.
>
> This is not to say that Christianity is finished. I am, on the contrary, convinced that *it is not Christianity but our conception and interpretation of it that has become antiquated in the present world situation.* The Christian symbol is a living thing that carries in itself the seeds of further development. It can go on developing; it depends only on us, whether we can make up our minds to meditate again,

more thoroughly, on the Christian premises. This requires a very different attitude towards the individual, towards the microcosm of the self.

Christianity holds at its core a symbol which has for its content the individual way of life of a man, the Son of Man, and that it even regards this individual process as the incarnation and revelation of God Himself... *Our denominational religions...express a view of the world (suitable) in the Middle Ages but...leave out of account all the mental developments of the last 500 years.*

Actually, Christianity has barely moved fifteen minutes past 1500 since it stopped thinking for itself and began to adopt from the secular.[10] Christianity needs to understand that God is sovereign in creation, sovereign in history, and will be sovereign in each individual—when and if that person accepts Him.

But Jung did not write his book until late 1950s, even after Bonhoeffer in the 1940s. So the influence of the earlier will philosophers continued during the entire twentieth century as Western civilization paddled toward the beacons of light shed by Masur's turn-of-the-century prophets. Their light beckoned the avant-garde intellectuals—especially during the two short decades between the two world wars.

Interim of Delusion

The interlude between the two world wars was truly an interim of delusion. At the helm during the interim were the avant-garde intellectuals personified by the Lost Generation.

---

10. Richard H. Tawney, *Religion and the Rise of Capitalism* (London: Murray, 1926). In speaking of the church during the Enlightenment, Tawney said, "An institution which does not think for itself adopts whatever is fashionable."

The Allies were deluded by victory after World War I, but losses outweighed gains. France lost the most since the war was fought on its soil. The loss of much property, a devastated no-man's-land, devalued currency, and a generation of manhood resulted in loss of the life spirit of France. Their *élan vital!*

Great Britain was deluded by thinking they could still rule the world and live in the manner and manor house to which they became accustomed in the nineteenth century, but they too lost the cream of young manhood. National debt was ten times the level of 1914, forty percent of their merchant fleet was sunk, and ties within the commonwealth were coming loose. Ireland and India loosened theirs.

The United States lost one hundred thousand men but actually benefited from the war as New York became a financial center equal to London. Heavy industry was stimulated by the war. The consumer industry was launched by Henry Ford, who wanted machines to free people from slavery. About the only victors who lost in America were those of the deluded Lost Generation.

For some Americans on their way home from World War I, a stopover in Paris was quite natural. *Vive la France!* At least the Left Bank suffered no loss of *élan*. It probably had more creativity per square foot than any other spot in the world. It was a mecca for talent, including an artistic band of self-imposed exiles from America, the Lost Generation.

Ernest Hemingway is a good example. He drove an ambulance in Italy during the war, stayed in Paris, joined the communist cause in Spain, went on safari in Africa beneath the snows of Kilimanjaro, and finally, as an old man, fished in the sea of the Caribbean. He sought the exotic in his quest for reality but never let the responsibility of everyday existence interfere with his self-indulgence. His *A Farewell to Arms* in 1929 expressed the position. An American soldier was hospitalized in Italy. His wound was not serious enough to interfere with the affair he had with the nurse who bore his child. By the time he recovered, the nurse and the child both had the good grace to die before he had to assume mundane responsibility for them. He had only to wallow gloriously in grief—though the moment was brief—then to go on footloose and free.

The United States, ever behind Europe in sophistication, had only a few spots that came close to this avant-garde Bohemianism. Yet some of the Lost Generation managed to take their sophistication home with them. Julian Hartt explained,[11]

> The Lost Generation did not all go on the bum in Europe after the Great War. Some of them managed the 'return to normalcy'. They came home to conventional marriages and had children, and worked at jobs, politics and occasionally at religion. But in their own way they fared badly, too. Theirs was a quiet non-histrionic, non-Bohemian damnation. (They throng the stories of F.Scott Fitzgerald and John O'Hara.) The burdens of 'normal life' are, of course, too much and too small for them and so they seek anesthesia in alcohol, sex, etc. But as the damned go they are rather ordinary people.

The rest of the United States was strictly *Main Street*, according to Sinclair Lewis. With hypocritical piety, these Americans enacted prohibition but worshipped the dollar, except for the Bible Belt, which never had many dollars to worship.

The farmers were also left behind in the prosperity that accompanied the shift from the farm to the city as urban population began to outnumber rural. But with the Great Depression, many people returned to the farm for subsistence.

---

11. Julian Hartt, *The Lost Image of Man* (Louisiana: Louisiana State University Press, 1963), 104.

The 1920s came to a crashing end when speculation ruined the stock market, overborrowing shorted the banks, financial manipulation undermined the economy, and protectionism stifled international trade. A chain reaction swept through the country with a run on the banks. Franklin Roosevelt swept into office, declared a bank holiday, went off the gold standard, and gradually reopened the banks. FDR assured people they had "nothing to fear but fear itself." This was consoling for those with jobs, but fourteen million people, a fourth to a third of the labor force, were unemployed. Soup lines grew long then were replaced with the alphabet soup of New Deal programs: AAA, CCC, NRA, NYA, PWA, WPA, etc., etc. Even so, it was the mobilization for World War II that finally broke the Depression.

Delusions never ceased. During the 1930s, some intellectuals signed the *Humanist Manifesto*. Others preferred the communist version and became fellow travelers on this wave of the future, for not only the USSR was deluded by Marxism. Yet to avoid communism, Germany accepted the delusions of Hitler's Nazi party. Italy accepted Mussolini's fascism. Japan followed its aggressive samurai war cabinet, which did not realize that imperialism was taboo after World War I.

Ironically, after the "war to make the world safe for democracy," the world moved in the opposite direction—toward communism, fascism, and totalitarianism. The United States was infiltrated with red agents and fifth-column Nazis as it sent scrap metal to Japan.

Deluded by appeasement talks in Europe, France and Britain awoke in 1939 when Hitler marched into Poland. Deluded by nonaggression talks with Japan, the United States awoke on December 7, 1941 when Japan bombed Pearl Harbor.

World War II was as inevitable as World War I was avoidable.

World War II

World War II was truly global. It began and ended in Manchuria. After the last empress dowager of the Manchu Dynasty died in China in 1911, reformers led by Sun Yat-sen began to modernize the country. Foreign ideas began to take root, as communism did. Foreign people tried to take root, as the Japanese did.

Japan became westernized by the end of the nineteenth century. As it shifted from an agrarian-feudal society to a commercial society, the samurai military caste lost its feudal place in society. The samurai took over the cabinet of advisors to the emperor after he bestowed a constitution with a bicameral diet. The samurai cabinet set Japan on a military course that was tested in the Russo-Japanese wars at the turn of the century.

Russia sought an all-weather port, but they were thwarted in the Black Sea by Britain in the Crimean War. They were stymied in the east by the loss of Port Arthur when Britain directed the peace negotiations held in New England that favored Japan. The peace undercut moderate Russians, such as Sergei Witte, who led the Russian delegation and tried to lead moderate reform in Russia. When moderates such as Witte lost the peace, anarchists took over and led Russia into the Bolshevik Revolution of 1917. After the moderates lost out, Americans believed Russians were either czarist autocrats or bomb-throwing anarchists.

Japan used the favorable peace terms to advantage. By 1931, Japan was ready to move into Manchuria for the coal and iron mines it needed. In 1937, Japan invaded China. They took over strategic cities such as Peiping, Canton, Shanghai. They built garrisons and controlled the railroads. Chiang Kai-shek, who succeeded Sun Yat-sen, was forced into southwest China while Mao Tse-tung's communists became entrenched in the northeast. Chiang Kai-shek was maintained during World War II with supplies from India via the Burma Road and the Flying Tiger airlift. Both were part of the southeastern theater of operations. After the war, Chiang Kai-shek was shoved off the mainland onto Taiwan as Mao Tse-tung extended his communist control throughout China.

Meanwhile in Europe, Hitler and Mussolini came to power in Germany and Italy on the pretext that they opposed communism. They did, but their Nazi and fascist ideas were just as bad. Hitler's concentration camps and his extermination of Jews were as bad as Stalin's gulags and purges. Hitler expanded his "ideas" into Europe with the *Anschluss* of Austria in the spring of 1938. By that fall, he moved into Czechoslovakia—after France and England agreed not to interfere with "self-determination." Czechoslovakia was chopped into pieces, which the Germans picked up in the spring of 1939. Poland was next, but Britain warned against the move. In order to avoid two fronts, Hitler signed a pact with Stalin that promised him part of Poland if Stalin did not intervene. Hitler marched into Poland. Britain and France declared war on September 3, 1939. World War II officially began.

Stalin immediately claimed his part of Poland, plus the Baltic countries of Estonia, Latvia, and Lithuania. He was slowed in Finland but annexed enough to secure Leningrad (St. Petersburg). Hitler quickly grabbed his part of Poland, plus Norway and Denmark.

While the pact with Stalin still held, Hitler moved west. In May 1940, Hitler confronted Britain and France, who just sat and waited for the half year since they declared war. They waited at the Maginot Line in France opposite the Siegfried Line in Germany. New concrete fortress bunkers on the Western Front were a far cry from the barbed-wire dirt trenches of World War I. They were impregnable.

Hitler merely swept around the end of the Maginot Line as he "blitzed" through Belgium and Holland. Both were unprotected and quickly capitulated. As German troops poured into northern

France, British and French troops evacuated from Dunkirk on anything that would float across the English Channel. A month later, in mid-June, German troops entered Paris. The French government fled south and set up the Vichy government, which collaborated with Germany. All of France was under Nazi control, except for the underground resistance movement. In London, with his Dunkirk evacuees, General Charles De Gaulle established the Western Front Free French government and trained for their return.

Hitler proposed peace with Britain. If Hitler could keep Europe, Britain would remain undisturbed on its island with their overseas empire. Winston Churchill was prime minister by then and not about to appease or surrender. Bombs began to fall on Britain. The United States stepped up its aid to Britain and to the Allies under a lend-lease system of accounting that ignored war debts.

After the fall of France, Japan spread into Southeast Asia— that is, into French Indo-China (Vietnam), also Thailand and Burma. Japan was ready to move into the Philippines and Australia. To insure success in the Philippines, still under US protection, Japan decided to cripple the US naval fleet and air force stationed at Pearl Harbor in Hawaii. Their attack on the morning of December 7, 1941 was a "day of infamy" that will live forever, Franklin Roosevelt told Congress as the United States declared war the next day.

The Philippines fell immediately. American troops were taken as prisoners of war. When General Douglas MacArthur was boated off the island, he promised, "I shall return." Australia was not invaded because America won the crucial Coral Sea naval battle. The domino fall of nations in Southeast Asia was finally halted. Australia became the center of Pacific operations as territory was slowly and painfully regained island by island. Weaker islands were taken first, leaving the Japanese stranded on islands that the Allies bypassed in their leapfrog move to Japan.

Back in Europe, as soon as Hitler took over France and put Britain under the blitz of air raids, he began a 1941 spring offensive to the Ukraine via the Balkans. Italy was bogged down in Greece and needed help on the way. Guerrilla action in Yugoslavia further delayed the Nazi march that spread through Eastern Europe from the Crimea and the Ukraine to the upper Don and Volga Rivers. Instead of pushing on to Moscow and Leningrad, Hitler concentrated on oil fields around Stalingrad (Volgograd) to relieve his short supply. The Soviets and the severe winter weather repelled the siege of the city. The Soviets then took the offensive and gradually pushed the Germans out of the USSR. (Strangely, as soon as Hitler turned on Stalin in the spring of 1941, the barrage of propaganda aimed at keeping the United States out of the war suddenly stopped.)

As Soviets took the offensive in Eastern Europe, the North African campaign began. German forces under Field Marshal Rommel were in Italian Libya and French Algiers. An Allied pincer movement was planned to close on Rommel. British forces under Bernard Montgomery in Egypt and American forces under Dwight Eisenhower in French Morocco advanced from opposite directions. By the time the pincer closed, the Allied forces ended up at Tunis, ready to hop across Sicily to Italy and take Italy out of the war. Tunis fell in May 1943. Sicily fell in July. Italy was out of the war by September 1944, although surrender was not official until Mussolini was executed by partisans in April 1945.

While Allies were busy in Italy, the USSR won back its western territory from the Ukraine to the Baltic. At this point, in December 1943, the Teheran Conference between Churchill, Roosevelt, and Stalin was held. The big three agreed to push toward Berlin from the east and the west after invasions were launched through north France at Normandy and through south France up the Rhone.

General Eisenhower was commander of the European Theater of Operations (ETO). He launched the Normandy invasion on D-Day, June 6, 1944. It was followed by the Battle of the Bulge led by General George Patton, who was ready to push on to Berlin. There was urgency to defeat Hitler before new war technology emerged. They already used unmanned missiles and were working on an atomic bomb.

Then came the Yalta Conference in February 1945, probably the most controversial of any the big three had. Roosevelt was a very sick man and in no condition to negotiate. He died two months later. Whether at Teheran or Yalta, Churchill gave up on his pet plan since World War I, which was to attack Germany and Austria through the Balkans via the Bosporus Straits and then claim the straits for Britain.

Instead, Stalin was allowed to take the Balkan route. Actually, the Balkans would have been liberated when Berlin collapsed. Stalin should have gone straight to Berlin, or he should have been ignored while Patton pushed the American drive to Berlin. During the wait, the Soviet detour of "liberation" through the Balkans secured those countries for the USSR, although it cost a million men and much delay. The forced delay of the American drive under Patton allowed the Soviets to reach Berlin at the same time as the Americans, so that half of Berlin and half of Germany fell to the Soviets.

Some historians say the concessions at Yalta were necessary to get Stalin to promise help in defeating Japan. But only after the atom bomb was dropped and the war was over did Soviet troops move into Manchuria. Thus, the war began and ended in Manchuria.

V-E Day (Victory in Europe) came on May 8, 1945. Hitler burned himself on a funeral pyre in the tradition of the pagan chieftains he admired. The Potsdam Conference was in late July and early August 1945. Harry Truman and Clement Attlee, successors of Roosevelt and Churchill, met with Joseph Stalin. They confirmed the Yalta agreements, even though Truman knew that the United States planned to drop two atom bombs in order to bring a quick end to the war, because an invasion of the Japanese mainland meant needless slaughter of American troops and many more Japanese.

The Japanese emperor surrendered on V-J Day, September 2, 1945. World War II ended, almost to the day six years after it officially began with the British and French declaration of war on September 3, 1939.

Peace after World War II was unique in the history of the world. Instead of reparations, unprecedented generosity on the part of the Americans rebuilt the defeated countries. General George Marshall devised the Marshall Plan that won the peace.

Actually, General Marshall was also instrumental in winning the war, in a behind-the-scenes sort of way. Between World War I and World War II, he updated the army for mobile warfare. He rewrote training manuals to institute realistic training. He retired older officers who could not adapt to the future and advanced capable young officers who could. During the six years of war (September 1939 to September1945), he built the army from a force of 174,000 to 8.3 million. But he never led any of them in battle. He was needed stateside by both presidents Roosevelt and Truman. When Truman asked him to serve as secretary of state, he envisioned the Marshall Plan. He reasoned that "democratic principles do not flourish on empty stomachs." Thus, he was instrumental in winning both the war and the peace.[12]

---

12. Information on General Marshall is from articles in *US News & World Report* (1998), which featured generals of the twentieth century. During World War I, General Pershing sent three hundred calvarymen into battle at Saint.-Mihiel. The horses panicked at the noise of machine guns and were now obsolete in war.

The Marshall Plan was one means used to defeat communism. The other was a policy of containment since the Cold War began as soon as World War II ended. The nations merely realigned themselves as the clash between two obsolete materialisms— dialectic and humanistic—continued for the rest of the century.

Hot spots flared: Korea in the 1950s, Vietnam in the 1960s, perpetually in the Middle East,[13] and in many other places— wherever people gathered.

Underlying Currents of Change

The big four of World War I became the big three during World War II and big two with peace.[14] There was talk of one world, but it went nowhere since that world had to be either red or red, white, and blue. Strangely, the world moved in the opposite direction— toward greater plurality as more nations gained independence and as the two superpowers lost dominance.

A different number given on the news in summer of 1998 showed sixteen million in the service during World War II. Of those who served, six million were still alive in 1998. World War II caused the death of sixty million people; most were civilians.

13. The establishment of Israel as a nation contributed to the unrest in the Middle East. The Balfour Declaration passed in the British Parliament approved the nation. After Word War I, the area was a British protectorate until the terrorism of Israelis ousted the British and the nation of Israel actually came into being after World War II.

Since imperialism was taboo after World War I, Britain and France used mandates and protectorates to get around it as they divided the Turkish Ottoman Empire in the Treaty of Versailles. In 2004, one news pundit commented that "Britain got the oil and France got the sand"— and the United States got the turmoil they left behind.

14. The big four were England, France, Italy, and the United States. The big three were England, the United States, and USSR. The big two were the United States and USSR.

Eric Hoffer, longshoreman and philosopher, observed that "dispersion of power is the only check to power there is." So with greater dispersion and diversity may come greater unity.

Max Ways noted two underlying supertrends, which seem opposite but are complementary:[15] 1) the trend toward more individuality, diversity, and plurality with more freedom and 2) the trend toward increasing interdependence of individuals, organizations, and nations. While these two invisible trends were evolving, the more visible Cold War was resolving itself.

Superseding all this, avant-garde intellectuals steadily advanced the ideas of those turn-of-the-century Euro prophets. The ideas finally reached the masses in the 1960s. Mass acceptance was accelerated because the baby boomers reaching college age were often the first generation of a family to attend college. So they were more vulnerable to avant-garde intellectuals without the tempering views of parents who were of the same college generation as the professors.[16] Thus, the '60s produced a generation of *nouveau intellectuals*—with intelligence such as the world had seldom seen before. All should be glad to benefit from their wisdom, in a repeat of the European attitude before World War I.

Paul Johnson explored this era from his British viewpoint. He now heads the list of generations of outstanding British historians that the island nation has produced. In his book *Intellectuals*, he identified many of the intellectuals who led us astray during the past century. He concluded that you cannot trust intellectuals.

---

15. Max Ways, *Fortune* (October 1970).
16. When I was in college during World War II and imparting newfound knowledge, my mother simply remarked, "Aren't you getting a little pink around the edges?" That was enough for me to rethink my "knowledge." She also wondered if the economics professor (known to them during their own college years) would like for his farm to be put in a collective. Too bad *nouveau intellectual* students of the 1960s had no such parents.

He also pointed out that in the last two hundred years, "secular intellectuals began to replace the old clerisy as guide and mentor of mankind." This is when the church stopped thinking for itself and adopted whatever was fashionable. The church left thinking to intellectuals—most of whom were atheists.

One of Johnson's intellectuals was Cyril Connolly. Oblivious to turmoil in the rest of the world, Cyril Connolly steadily advanced the turn-of-the-century agenda in Britain. He was born in 1903 and somehow missed the sobering reality of World War I, the Depression of the '30s, and World War II of the '40s. Instead, he began a progressive pursuit of "enlightened hedonism." During the '20s (when he was in his twenties), he called the pursuit "perfection in happiness." In the '30s, he called it "aesthetic materialism." In the '40s, he took up the "defense of civilized standards" that had ten aims, whereby every person was entitled to free food, clothes, medicine, light, heat, and water—just like the free air they breathed.[17]

When some of the extremes that Connolly proposed reached the masses during the fateful 1960s, they led to irresponsibility and unrestricted abandon, which became the formula for a permissive anything-goes society.

The cult of *violence* was added to the brew when Jean-Paul Sartre (b. 1905) argued,

> When youth confronts the police, our job is not only to show that it is the police who are the violent ones but to join youth in counter-violence.

Norman Mailer (b. 1923) latched onto Sartre when he asked, "Might not personal violence sometimes, for some people, be necessary and even virtuous?" In his 1957 book *The White Negro*,

---

17. Paul Johnson, *Intellectuals* (London: Weidenfeld & Nicolson, 1989), 316.

he presented the case of the beating death of a sweetshop owner by two young men. Did it not have its beneficial aspect?

> One murders not only a weak 50-year old man, but an institution as well, (though) one violates private property, one enters into a new relation with the police and introduces a dangerous element into one's life.[18]

Thus, personal violence opposed to the "institutionalized violence" of society was "good." This was used to justify the violent demonstrations against the institutionalized violence of the Vietnam War. It inspired Jerry Rubin, Abbie Hoffman, the Black Panthers, and others. Paul Johnson observed:

> Mailer epitomized the inter-threading of permissiveness with violence which characterized the '60s and '70s.[19]

Paul Johnson and his classmate Kenneth Peacock Tynan were born in 1927, too young for World War II, so they went straight to Oxford where Tynan embraced hedonism. After Oxford, he produced plays and reviews. His motto was, "Write heresy, pure heresy." He had much influence on the world theater. Johnson stated that "no one in Britain played a bigger role in destroying the old system of censorship, formal and informal." Tynan's "uncensored" life brought its own destruction.[20]

The self-censoring Hays office in Hollywood cleaned up the risqué 1920s. In 1939, it had to approve Rhett Butler's "Frankly, my dear, I don't give a *damn*" in *Gone with the Wind*. By the 1960s, US self-censoring went the way of Britain's. (Oh, for a few innocent *damn*s in place of what we have now.)

---

18. Ibid., 318.
19. Ibid., 322–324.
20. Ibid., 325–327.

Three themes of '60s culture were 1) uninhibited sex, 2) violence, 3) drugs. Another ingredient was "victimhood," which James Baldwin furthered. Baldwin went to Harlem schools when "there was no race-conscious defeatism. [Instead] the belief was that blacks, if they worked hard enough, could excel."[21]

Baldwin thrived with help from many teachers and became a success. But when victimhood became fashionable, he claimed that he was a deprived, bullied, and mistreated "victim."

> [Baldwin] reinforced Sartre's rhetoric that violence was the legitimate right of those who could be defined by race, class or predicament, to be the victims of moral iniquity.[22]

Or claim to be victims of merely "perceived inequity."

At a time when ideas are so at odds with sanity and reality, crisis is bound to ensue that will overturn the idiocy.

In that distant century that mirrored ours, as it turned to 1500, such a crisis period of righting began—not because the powers-that-be came to their senses but in spite of them. Because the providence of history and the underlying law of balance and sanity prevail in the end. In the meantime, mankind, with its after-the-fact politics, can do a very effective job of tipping the scales to delay sanity, thereby causing more pain than is necessary.

In a Sea of Chaos

During the twentieth century, Western civilization moved headlong into chaos. So what now? Now that Western civ has spread throughout the world—at least technologically. And now that the number seven civilization has remained the "little while" allotted in Revelation. And now that the West is showing symptoms of decline.

---

21. Ibid., 334.
22. Ibid., 337.

Western civilization has turned through its civilization cycle to the point of disintegration. W. Warren Wagar presented Sorokin's analysis of the civilization cycle:

> Sorokin distinguishes three major phases in the life-cycle of cultural super-systems. In the (idealistic) phase, ultimate reality is defined as absolute spirit or deity, and truth is regarded as above reason and above the senses [during the Christian Middle Ages].
>
> In the Sensate phase, its dialectical opposite, ultimate reality is defined as the tangible material world revealed to the sense organs [West since Enlightenment]. Between the two extremes is the (ideational) or *integral* phase... with a balanced rational synthesis of both (idealistic) and sensate reality and knowledge.[23]

We will move into the "integral" stage in the coming *age of integrity*. That is when we put our fragmented ideas back together with wisdom, honesty, and integrity—the integrity of each idea, each individual, an integral part of the whole of all society and all creation—through a metaphysical framework of knowledge.

At present, Western civ still lingers in the last gasps of the sensate.

> The West is in the twilight of a sensate phase which at best produced Shakespeare, Rubens, Goethe, and Beethoven; but is now capable of only the vulgar, crude, flamboyant or at most the brilliantly incoherent eclectic. The rise of

---

23. W. Warren Wagar, *The City of Man* (Boston: Houghton Mifflin, 1963), 93. Actually, *idealistic* and *ideational* have been exchanged in this quote (as in the parentheses). *Idealistic* seems more applicable to a stage that regarded truth as transcendent and beyond man's reason as in the Middle Ages while *ideational* seems more applicable to ideas that arise from experience and include intuitive insight of a higher source—thus, a synthesis of the other two.

dictatorships, crime, warfare, imperialism, profiteering, divorce, suicide, mental illness and the complete breakdown of value spring inevitably from the bankruptcy of sensate culture. Since *the previous system of value is disintegrated and a new system not yet built, we are faced with social, mental and moral anarchy.*[24]

Wagar completed his analysis as he identified the main crisis of our time:

The crisis of our age is primarily the disunity of science and in a larger sense, the total failure of all the knowledge-seeking disciplines, the human sciences even more than the natural, to produce a single unified picture of the phenomenal world. Like the pieces of a jigsaw puzzle scattered in confusion over a tabletop, the separate sciences do not make a coherent whole, although with effort, they could.[25]

The result is that no one mind has anything like a connected picture of the world. Much knowledge goes to waste, many fruitful inter-relationships are never explored, and we are faced with conceptual chaos...Disciplines overlap and fail to mesh...to our staggering glut of knowledge must be added the super-problem of how to fit the knowledge we have into a *metaphysical framework* big enough to hold it. Here, chaos is even more universal. Methods of modern science offer no help. Philosophers long ago abandoned the search for frameworks.[26]

And sadly, theologians have followed the secular lead instead of providing the metaphysical framework that people need. And only theologians can provide.

---

24. Ibid., 94.
25. Ibid., 95.
26. Ibid., 174.

Such a framework would also provide the insight needed to complete the fulfillment of the three revolutions set in motion by the Reformation with Galileo, Columbus, and Luther. But we are beset with conceptual chaos instead.

1. Science-technology, evolving since Galileo, has finally freed man from physical-economic bondage. Thanks to machines, ours is the first time in history that civilization can exist without a slave base. However, new physics and new science have left us with concepts that are too deep to understand in common, everyday language. Thus, we are left with conceptual chaos.

2. Through Columbus's discovery of America, the United States was founded and found the way to freedom from sociopolitical bondage, as expressed in the Declaration of Independence. But this has not yet been fulfilled because we still try to export democracy and human rights without the reformed Judeo-Christian base, so the conflict between humanistic and dialectic materialism continued to the end of the twentieth century. We have not yet emerged from our social chaos.

3. The individual-ideational-spiritual revolution, which began with Luther and the Reformation's priesthood of the believer—the idea of each person thinking for himself—should bring us conceptual freedom. During our turbulent twentieth century, we definitely found our individuality, but we lost the spiritual and ended with our concepts in complete chaos.

So we end a fractured century with a disintegrating civilization in a sea of conceptual chaos. Or as Revelation put it—"the harlot civilization…is riding the beast of knowledge…in a sea of chaos."

7

A View of the Whole

Overall Worldview

A number of years ago, the president of a college[1] commented that the students were given many bits and pieces of knowledge with differing views of the world. At 9:00 a.m., they went to natural-science class with one view of the world. At 11:00 a.m., they went to sociology with another view. At 1:00 p.m., they went to religion with yet another view. But they received no comprehensive overall view anywhere.

This is the conceptual chaos Warren Wagar identified as the crisis of our age. Bits and pieces of knowledge are scattered like the pieces of a jigsaw puzzle, but we do not have an overall picture to guide us in putting it together. We do not have the picture on the puzzle-box top. Theology can and must provide the metaphysical framework that the students need, which we all need. For a

---

1. Harry Smith of Austin College (Presbyterian) in Sherman, Texas.

connected overall view of the world—that is commonly held—is what holds civilization together and will be the salvation of our worldwide society.

Wilhelm Dilthey (1830–1900) emphasized the importance of a worldview (*Weltanschauung*) and a world picture (*Weltbild*)— the picture on the puzzle-box top. He felt that a study of history provided a worldview that raised one above one's own civilization. Europeans desperately needed this when he wrote just before the turn of the twentieth century. His study of history revealed three different worldviews:

1. Cosmic of Hellenic civilization
2. Social of Roman with its law
3. Religious of the West with its Judeo-Christian tradition

These three views may be brought together for the comprehensive overall view of the world that is needed. The metaphysical framework will include the cosmic of all creation (for that 9:00 a.m. class), the social of all mankind and all history (for that 11:00 a.m. class), and the spiritual of a fulfilled Judeo-Christian tradition (for that 1:00 p.m. class). Thus, a *fulfilled* Judeo-Christian religion will provide the metaphysical framework that is needed to hold the world together.

How is this possible? Gerald Heald identified man's present religious dilemma.

> What the world needs is a three-ply religion ministering to man's three great religious needs, only one of which is well served by any single positive faith.[2]

1. Identity with nature as in Chinese oriental religion
2. A revealed code of ethics, plus the humanity and love of Christianity

---

2. Gerald Heald cited in Wagar, *The City of Man*, 161–166.

3. Spiritual exercises for the integration of the self, as in Buddhism and Eastern religions

We must also remember that there is only one God Almighty, then acknowledge that He is sovereign in all three areas.

Syncretism is not the solution, even though British historian Arnold Toynbee seemed to lean in that direction. Georg Hegel saw that all religions go through the same three stages: from nature gods, to ethical and social morality, then to the spiritual. Both Toynbee and Hegel provided insight but fell short of what is needed.

The answer is the most simple, most obvious thing in the world. The Trinity concept, evolved through the Judeo-Christian tradition, is just waiting to be fully understood. *One* God: Creator, Christ, Holy Spirit.

The Creator and His Creation

First, we must realize that any people, anywhere, anytime, have been able to conceive of Creator and Spirit. God would certainly have given that comfort to all people. Various cultures built religious systems on either one or both. Using both, the American Indians developed a natural religion that some people felt lacking in organized religion of the twentieth century.

This is because we neglect God the Creator, but the earth will sing when we reinstate the Creator and His creation. Paul said, "Creation waits with eager longing for the revealing of the sons of God" (Rom 8:19). The earth groans for the day of man's redemption, when there will be harmony between man and creation.

The earth has waited ever since Noah, when mankind was separated from creation and God promised never again to curse the ground because of man (Gen. 8:21). Moral reckoning was henceforth between man and man: "Whoever sheds blood of man, by man shall his blood be shed" (Gen. 9:6). Man was separated from creation, but God and creation remained in accord. Creation obeys and works according to God's laws of nature. God *is* sovereign in His creation.

In order to really understand this, people must remain close to creation themselves. Separate yet one. It was in the hinterlands that God revealed Himself to the patriarchs (Abraham, Isaac, Jacob) as El Shaddai, God Almighty, *one* God of all creation. After Israel's exodus from Egypt, they wandered forty years in the wilderness, partly to wash out their excess civilization and to renew their closeness to the Creator and His creation. By the time they reached the Promised Land, they knew it was God's land and they were merely stewards. Their land-ownership laws reflected this.

Psalms and Isaiah reiterate over and over the greatness and glory of God's creation and His sovereignty in His creation.

When people lose this feeling of closeness and oneness with God and His creation, as they have repeatedly ever since Babel (which is ever since civilization began), God has brought them back down to earth through the *fall* of civilization. This happened to every civilization, including the six in the Judeo-Christian line of ascent. But what about number seven?

During the Enlightenment in Europe, Western civilization separated from creation and from God. Europeans felt their separation from creation, but not from God, so they came up with those mixed-up, nature-society ideas—man is by nature free, yet free of nature—which produced Rousseau's natural education and Gauguin's search for a primitive South Seas paradise. During all of this, Americans retained a natural closeness to creation and to God, at least on each last new frontier that opened.

But what now—now that the last frontiers of America and all over the world are being despoiled by overcivilization? Will number seven fall? Or come to its senses and come to acknowledge God the Creator?

In Revelations 21, John saw "in the vision of salvation the old earth despoiled by sin is replaced by a glorious new earth appropriate for God's redeemed people." But this will not happen unless and until there is a change in attitude toward God's creation. The present ecology bit is a step in the right direction but still lacks the vision to see and to truly understand that the world, the universe, is *God's creation*.

God's Spirit moved over the "deep" to create order out of physical chaos and has kept order ever since. Science helps us understand the laws of God's creation so we may work in harmony with them. But when Western civilization separated the natural and social sciences, natural science was used to subdue and exploit nature for the sake of humanity, which was enshrined in place of God. The churches felt threatened by natural science, so they left creation to science and took humanism for theology. They ignored a worldview and took only a human-life view.

For example, when Albert Schweitzer developed his "reverence for life" theology, he divorced *life view* from *worldview* and separated belief in a divine pattern and providence from belief in goodness and gentleness. He reasoned that

> One could be agnostic about the design of the universe and still find significance and the foundation of ethics in man.[3]

On the other hand, Albert Einstein accepted the divine pattern. He acknowledged the cosmic God of the universe, but Einstein did not accept one who concerned himself with the petty affairs of man and history.

---

3. James Brabazon, review of Albert Schweitzer, *Houston Chronicle*, 1975.

Both fell short of the all-encompassing picture of the world that we need. Man can no longer afford such shortsighted cleavage in his views. For contrary to what the good Dr. Schweitzer thought, man cannot neglect the divine pattern of creation. Nor is the cosmic God of Einstein enough, for this neglects the providence of God in history.

The Turning Point

Fortunately, that is not all there is. Ever since Moses, God has revealed His providence in history through the unique sense of history that He gave to the Hebrews. They traced their begats back to the dawn of history, even to the dawn of creation. They also traced their trek through the developing and expanding spiral of five Medi-East civilizations when each was dominant.

At that point, at the turning point of history and of creation, God sent His Son. As Owen Barfield explained,[4]

> The blind-spot which posterity will find most startling in the last hundred years or so of Western civilization, is that it had, on the one hand, a religion which differed from all others in its acceptance of time, and of a particular point in time, (Christ) as a cardinal element in its faith; that it had, on the other hand, a picture in its mind of the history of the earth and man as an evolutionary process; (yet) neither saw nor supposed any connection between the two.
>
> One would have expected those who accepted evolution and remained Christians, to see the incarnation of their Savior as the culminating point of history of the

---

4.   Barfield, *Saving the Appearances*, 167–168.
   Owen Barfield saw a connection between Christ's "point in time" and all creation. "There will be a revival of Christianity when it becomes impossible to write a popular manual of science without referring to the Incarnation of the Word" (p. 164).

earth—a turning-point of time…(we are) hardly past (so) hardly know…what the Incarnation means; for what is 2000 years in comparison with the ages which preceded it?

We may now recall the remarkable phrases that run through the first verses of Genesis and are still ahead of science: "separating and gathering."

Ever since God "spoke" at creation, there has been an overall thrust to separation within which the separating and gathering stages of cumulative development unfolded.[5] The overall

---

5. This *may* be the key to the unified field theory that Einstein sought and others still seek. If we can find the solution in these few simple words— "separating and gathering together"—this will be another example of "The Word Unsealed." These words are certainly the key to a *concept* that is understandable in everyday, common-sense terms.

First, think of the overall separating, expanding, thrust force that is called the big bang. Then think of its opposite, an overall gathering-together, collapsing, gravitational force. These two underlying forces are now known as dark energy and dark matter. Next, imagine that both of these overall forces are composed of tiny, tiny bits of energy because the smaller the bits, the more design possibilities there are. For convenience, let's call these tiniest bits of energy *plus* (+) and *minus* (-). Then imagine how the bits separated and gathered together into larger bits in *cumulative* stages of development within the overall thrust of the big bang (i.e., of dark energy).

When tiny plus (+) bits of thrusting energy separated at the beginning of the cumulative thrust (the big bang), their energy was quickly spent. They would have collapsed through the "gravity" of the gathering-together force of dark matter, except that they were quickly joined by more and more thrusting separating bits of energy at tremendous speed. The new and old plus and minus energy bits gathered together into strings, quarks, etc. As they held one another in complementary balanced suspension, they were slowed and stabilized.

Energy slowed evolves into matter. $M = E/C^2$. This was Einstein's original formula that later became $E = MC^2$. *Matter* is energy slowed

thrust began with dark energy that pushes things—pushes the universe—apart and dark matter that pulls things together. These two underlying forces first separated and gathered together on the nuclear level of sub-subatomic energy waves and particles.

---

down, while *energy* is matter speeded up—both in relation to the speed of light squared, C^2.

The slowed bits of energy were joined by more and more thrusting separating bits of energy, which produced more gathering together with more slowing and stabilizing. Protons, electrons, etc., evolved at the subatomic level of development.

Protons in the nucleus of an atom have a thrusting, separating force, which keeps their companion electrons in orbit. Electrons (with a gathering, gravity-type force) circle the nucleus, herding the protons together—somewhat like a sheepdog circles the sheep to hold them together. The thrusting of the protons and the gathering together of the encircling electrons are the *strong* and *weak* nuclear forces that operate within the atom.

The only electromagnetic wave we can see with our eyes is *light*. Magnetic forces are also recognized in bar magnets with positive and negative ends. Like ends push apart and repel each other while opposite ends attract and draw together. In this way, positive and negative forces operate between atoms and molecules to form matter on the chemical level of development. Greater masses of matter draw together and accumulate through gravity (i.e., through the gathering-together force of dark matter).

Gravity is the force that we recognize in the overall gathering-together force of dark matter. It is the opposite and complement of the overall thrusting, separating force—the big bang pushed by dark energy. Ultimately, matter gathers together with increasing speed as it is drawn into black holes. So the forces we recognize at different levels of development are the nuclear weak and strong, electromagnetic, and dark-energy and dark-matter. All three are simply separating and gathering together at different levels of development within the universe—thus, one *unified* system of balanced separating and gathering together.

When God said, "Let there be light," He created electromagnetic waves. After the subnuclear, He separated and gathered together on the astrochemical level, then on the astrophysical and geophysical levels, and finally, on the biophysical level of cells that ultimately produced man.

The "separations" continued in social evolution: With Adam, mankind separated from God. With Noah, mankind was separated from creation. With Abraham, an individual separated his tribe from society, from mankind.

With Christ, the overall thrust of separation has changed to the unity of all things in heaven and earth—that is, toward "gathering together." Paul explained,

> For God has made known to us…His will…set forth in Christ as a plan for the fullness of time, to *unite* all things in him, things in heaven and things on earth. (Eph. 1:9–10, RSV)

With imagination, the Incarnation may be seen in relation to our cosmic turning point. British cosmologist Stephen Hawking once observed,

> One of the most amazing things is that the universe should be so close to the dividing line between expanding [separating] and collapsing [gathering together].[6]

Most scientists now think the universe will keep on expanding. No one really knows, so we may or may not be at the cosmic turning point. But we can see that the separation and proliferation of civilizations during BC centuries has changed in AD centuries to the unity and gathering together into one worldwide civilization.

Throughout the world, we have the same body of fragmented knowledge, the same conceptual chaos. We now need the cohesion

---

6. "Probing the Universe," *Newsweek* (March 12, 1979): 50.

of a connected, commonly held, and commonly understood overall view of the world to hold knowledge and society together.

The Metaphysical Framework

For the metaphysical framework needed, all knowledge may be loosely fitted under the three parts of the Trinity.

But knowledge must not be equated with a Person of the Trinity. And we must not think that the Persons of the Trinity had a consecutive designated time slot to fill—that the Creator did his bit, then Christ, and then the Holy Spirit. All were with God in the beginning, are now, and ever shall be. John introduced his gospel, "In the beginning was the Word, and the Word was with God, and the Word was God" (John1:1, RSV).

The Word is God's Spirit that created, that became flesh, and that is available to each spiritual individual. God is not time limited. Only our understanding is limited. So God revealed Himself in stages, as man became conscious enough to comprehend. Perhaps now we may be able to see the whole framework with its many interrelations.

Creator	Christ in History	Spirit in the Individual
physical creation (physical evolution from subnuclear to the bio-physical)	social history (social evolution including all of man's accumulated fund of knowledge)	spiritual individuals (each one is a microcosm of development—physical, social, and spiritual, e.g., Embryos repeat eons of physical evolution.)
Creator	Christ in History	Spirit in the Individual
natural science	social science	theology, philosophy, psychology

natural law	moral law, ethics	law of individual integrity
creation relation	social relation	spiritual relation to God (of each individual)
heredity	environment	will
As set forth in the American Declaration of Independence		
Creator	Providence	Judge (the inner judgment of spiritual integrity)
As in the three Revolutions set in motion by the Reformation, represented by three men:		
Galileo	Columbus	Luther
science-technology	social-political	spiritual-ideational

Now we can see the whole chain of evolution that has come down to each of us through God's spirit at work in all of creation, at work in society (all of history), and ultimately, at work in the spiritual individual, *the* Christ, who was conceived by and filled with the Holy Spirit and took mankind into the spiritual realm.

If we understand the flow of evolution from creation to society to the individual, it helps us see the framework and the underlying interrelated unity. This interrelated unity will become more apparent later in the section on the age of integrity.

For students to understand this, they need to be instructed with a curriculum based on the metaphysical framework. They need a simple but basic grounding in the natural sciences, also in social science based on history, plus a theology-philosophy-psychology combination that admits a spiritual component in each individual and acknowledges God. Then students will have a well-rounded education, and they will not get conflicting views in their classes at 9:00 a.m., 11:00 a.m., and 1:00 p.m.

Also, all people will move toward a commonly-held worldview that will be the salvation of society and the world.

The Flow of Evolution

For a theological understanding of the metaphysical framework, we need to see the Lord Jesus in the flow of evolution from creation through society to this unique spiritual individual *at* and *as* the turning point of creation, of history, and of each individual.

Eons of physical evolution led to ages of social and spiritual evolution before *the* Christ—the unique spiritual *individual*—took mankind into the spiritual realm. Now the Holy Spirit may truly dwell in each individual person, as it did in Christ, to bring each individual to oneness with God.

Christ showed the way. He is the way to spiritual oneness with God. When he prayed in the Garden of Gethsemane, "not my will, but Thy will be done," he merged his will with God's will and affirmed his spiritual oneness with God. When he died on the cross, he opened the way to the spiritual kingdom of God, for the veil that separated man from God was torn away—just as the curtain in the temple was torn away. Now each person—through *a* Christ event in his own Gethsemane—may merge his will with God's will and say yes to God and affirm his spiritual oneness with Him, the way *the* Christ opened the way.

Incidentally, this is our one real choice in life. Ever since free will was given to mankind (to Adam and Eve), we can say yes or no to God. On that one basic choice, all our other choices depend. Adam and Eve were the first to have the choice, when consciousness and freedom were given to mankind

According to Sartre, "Consciousness and freedom are given together. The essential freedom, the ultimate and final freedom that cannot be taken from a man, is to say 'No.'" Sartre felt that man's ultimate choice is to say no to life and commit suicide.[7] This may be a person's ultimate choice *if* he does *not* say yes to God and affirm life.

When freewilled Adam said no to God and ate of the tree, he separated from God and became self-conscious. He recognized the otherness of God, but he failed to retain his spiritual oneness, his sameness with God. So man has been groping ever since, not always knowing for what he searches. Yet God's Spirit has reached *out* to and *into* more and more people so that all may know Him and be one with Him. The Bible is the cumulative narrative of God's continuing revelation of Himself as man was able to understand. Finally, God sent His Son, who took away the last veil of separation. Now God's Spirit may dwell in all of us—Christ's way—so each person, by his own free-will choice, may consciously affirm his spiritual oneness with God.

Each person is a microcosm of the divine pattern. Each person, in the womb before he is born, repeats eons of physical evolution. It is amazing how much the embryos of various vertebrates (fish, salamander, tortoise, chicken, rabbit, man) resemble one another at a very early *shrimplike* stage of development.[8]

After he is born, each child repeats the stages of social and spiritual evolution as he reaches out into the world—to society (people around him) and to creation. A child of two to three

---

7.   William Barrett, *Irrational Man,* 1958, Doubleday, p.214-215

In Emil Brunner's 'crisis theology' God confronts man. Man can say 'No' to God and turn to death or he can say 'yes' and become a new man. Wm. Hordern, *Layman's Guide to Protestant Theology,* MacMillan, 1968, p.119 ...Brunner (Swiss, 1889-1966) did not really 'discover' crisis theology, for it was evident ever since Abraham's 'Fear and Trembling' at the sacrifice of Isaac, ever since Jacob's wrestling, ever since Moses' burning bush, on through the Bible even to Christ's temptations–and now in each person's life.

8.   Richard M. Tullar, *Life:Conquest of Energy* (New York: Holt, Rinehart and Winston, 1971), 307.

"names" the way generic man did as he learns to talk. At five, he becomes self-conscious, as Adam did.

In fact, we experienced a five-year-old child's repeat of Adam eating of the Tree of Knowledge. When our older son was five, he announced one night at prayer time, "I don't think I'll believe in God."

"Hmm. Why not?'

"'Because I can't understand all about Him."

"Well, I'm glad I can't understand all about Him. He wouldn't be much of a God if I could understand all about him."

And yet many intelligent grown people think like this five-year-old. (Incidentally, bedtime is also a good time to review good parts of the day, especially if the day had some rough spots. A child should be able to go to sleep *happy* with himself and his world.)

At seven to eight, a child's reasoning begins for a sense of right and wrong, as after Noah. Then he begins religious understanding at the Abraham level, but children are still little Jacobs who try to get by with anything they can. At ten to twelve, they like to set rules for their games. This is the Moses stage when they really want and need rules and limits, including the Ten Commandments. Actually, they need the Ten Commandments from this age through the teen and young-adult years, for it takes much maturity and judgment, with an indwelling of the Holy Spirit, before a person has the integrity to live as Jesus commanded.

Jesus's two commands were, "The Lord your God is one God." The Lord is *one* God sovereign in creation, sovereign in history, and sovereign in each individual who gives his "whole" person to God. For you shall "Love the Lord your God with ALL your heart, strength, mind and soul" (Mark 12:30, NIV). A *whole* person *at one* with God is at peace with himself, affirms himself, loves himself. Only such a positive person can truly reach out to his neighbor with love and understanding, which will then ripple throughout the world.

Any person, any individual—ever since Christ—has been able to enter the spiritual kingdom of God and to have spiritual oneness with God. But for mankind as a whole, the spiritual kingdom has not yet arrived. In fact, Western civilization had to turn through its civilization cycle before *mankind* could be taken over the Reformation threshold. So we keep praying, "Thy kingdom come."

Ideational Spiritual Growth

Mankind as a whole is now poised to cross the Reformation threshold. Each spiritual individual is truly able to think for himself. But in our present crisis of conceptual chaos, this is more like standing on the brink of a threshold chasm. In order to step across the abyss of our knowledge gap—and glut—we need to sort through the pieces and build a bridge of understanding to reach fulfillment on the other side. Then ideational-spiritual man, developing since Adam and Eve first nibbled of the Tree of Knowledge, may finally come into being.

When Adam and Eve nibbled and thought, consciously and self-consciously, they separated from God. Thus began man's journey from his common origin in Genesis, when he was *unconsciously* one with God, to his common destiny in Revelation when he will *consciously* be one with God again.

So where are we now? What has happened since the Reformation that should bring about its fulfillment? The New World was "discovered" just in time to provide a refuge for Protestants so that a new-world spirit might evolve and be fulfilled. This new-world spirit, which began in the climate of the times around the Reformation, had three thrusts of development represented by three men, as already mentioned.

1. Galileo. For since his use of the lens, science-technology developed and freed man from *physical-economic* bondage through machines and American-style capitalism.
2. Columbus. For he discovered America where the United States freed man from *sociopolitical* bondage with its Declaration of Independence.
3. Luther. For with the Reformation taken to the United States, where each person is truly able to think for himself, mankind will finally be freed from *conceptual* bondage.

The idea of Americans bringing conceptual freedom to mankind is rather ironic. In the 1950s, Father Bruckberger pointed out that Americans were *not yet* intellectually independent of European thought. In the 1980s, Alan Bloom felt we were still influenced too much by German philosophers. In 2003, a college professor sent a letter to the editor of *The Wall Street Journal* in which he stated, "All colleges—high and low—are anti-intellectual to the max these days."[9]

William Barrett noted,

> Americans are not only *non*-intellectual but *anti*-intellectual...In America a philosophical idea is an alien and embarrassing thing.[10]

Even ministers subscribe to this when they say we have too much theology.

Owen Barfield quoted the bishop of Plymouth (in his letter to *The Times* in London in the early 1960s):

---

9. Alan Bloom, *The Closing of the American Mind* (New York: Simon & Schuster, 1987). The name of the professor and date of his letter to *The Wall Street Journal* has been lost.
10. William Barrett, *Irrational Man* (New York: Anchor Books, 1962), 238.

> Our Lord emphasized his healing ministry to the whole man; if he is not Lord of our minds, he is not the savior whom this generation…so sorely needs.

Barfield then observed,

> I am persuaded that in our time the battle between the powers of good and evil is pitched in man's mind even more than in his heart, since it is known that the latter will ultimately follow the former.[11]

Maybe we are supposed to use the minds God gave us. Maybe God did bring Reformation refugees to America for a purpose. For a new-world spirit!

New-World Spirit Fulfilled

We have already seen how the reformed Judeo-Christian background in America, especially New England, influenced the Declaration of Independence. Jonathan Edwards of New England inspired a "great awakening" during the 1700s. This spread through the mid-Atlantic states but did not reach the South until the mid-1800s. The South was the least religious area in 1850 before the Civil War but the most religious since.

When Unitarians became strong in New England, Thomas Jefferson predicted they would also become dominant in the South. Exactly the opposite happened. Perhaps in reaction to Unitarianism, the denominations that did evangelize the South overstressed the divinity of Christ, almost forgetting his humanity. Of course, Christianity has swung from one extreme to the other ever since its inception. Christianity had to stress the Second Person of the Trinity in order to become established in

---

11. Barfield, *Saving the Appearances*, 165.

the first place. The Second Person has been dominant because all authority was given to Christ, and he sat at the right hand of God. He was at the forefront leading history. But as Christianity spread into the South, new interpretations arose that overemphasized the divinity of Christ.

Some of the first to move south were New England Congregationalists. Baptists also arrived in the south. Although Baptists remained separate bodies for the most part, their dedication and enthusiasm in evangelism never lagged.

The Anglican Church of England became the Episcopal Church in the United States after the American Revolution but did not reach out either place. Methodists became the evangelizing arm of the Church of England. In 1730, Montesquieu observed there was very little religion in England. About that same time, the Wesley brothers, John and Charles, began study groups "spreading Scriptural holiness over the land." They rode their horses to spread holiness to every hamlet. The Sunday-school movement began. They formed societies, held conferences, and in 1836, Methodists separated from the Church of England. They spread to America, especially to the South. Like the Wesleys, circuit-riding preachers spread the scripture to the unchurched on the frontiers.

Presbyterians, mainly from Scotland and Northern Ireland, settled in areas from New England to the Carolinas. Ever since Calvin and the Reformation, they insisted on well-educated ministers so they immediately established colleges, such as Princeton in 1746. Their early start in evangelism, when they sent trained ministers to outlying unchurched areas, helped them become one of the leading denominations in the United States— until the Civil War split the denomination.

Civil War and Reconstruction, to say nothing of economic policies before and after the war, doomed the South to another century as a "colonial," agrarian hinterlands. Since it retained

THE RIGHT HAND OF GOD

its closeness to creation—and had few dollars to worship—it remained the last bastion of religion in America. The Bible Belt.

In addition to this, Texas remained the last frontier settled by large groups of immigrants from Europe, even into the twentieth century. They brought their Lutheran strain of Protestantism. So while the South retained its overreaction to Unitarianism (anathema since Calvin allowed Servetus to be burned at the stake), Texas was infused with Europeans who had a more balanced concept of the Trinity and emphasized one God Almighty. A beloved, all-powerful God. *Der Liebe Gott.*

The Trinity will remain fragmented and unbalanced until we see one God, His sovereignty, and His revelation in the flow of evolution. This is seen in the neglect of the Creator by all Christians and in the overemphasis of spiritualism by others. Recognizing God and His sovereignty in all areas provides wholeness and balance to the Trinity. Thus, a whole religion of whole individuals in a whole society in a whole world! *Whole* means both complete and sound.

Theologians of the twentieth century did not stress a whole religion. In fact, William Hamilton concluded, "Theology must become humble and fragmentary, (and) dare not claim knowledge to develop a systematic description of the whole of life."[12] Twentieth-century theologians obliged by adding fragments to theology—but how dare we *not* see what God reveals?

Karl Barth (Swiss, born 1886) was shocked by World War I and despaired of theologians, so he turned to the Bible. (When all else fails, read the directions.) He told students to

> read the Bible with one hand and the newspaper with the other...because theology needs constant reform... to relate the Word of God to the age. (But) not even the

---

12. William E. Hordern, *A Layman's Guide to Protestant Theology* (London: MacMillan Co., 1968), 241.

Bible can be identified with the Word of God. The error of fundamentalism is that it takes the Bible as a "self-sufficient Paper-Pope."[13]

So Barth built theology around the act of God in Christ. Thus the Word of God Incarnate superseded the written Word of God, according to Barth and his followers. But what about the Word of God in creation? And how would we know anything about the Word Incarnate without the written Word of the Bible? The Bible does become an idol when we do not see beyond the "word" to God. Also when, because of too-literal interpretations, we do not see beyond the words, the parables, and the symbolism to the truth of God's message—and to God Himself.

Paul Tillich (born in Prussia, 1886–1965) felt that "to Protestantism only God is holy, and no church, no doctrine, no saint, no institution, no rite, is holy in itself...(but) points beyond itself to God."[14]

Even the Trinity points beyond itself to God, for the Trinity is the manifestation of God's Spirit—God's Word—at work in creation, at work in *the* Christ of history, and at work in each spiritual individual who accepts God's Spirit as Christ did.

Tillich saw the world and Christ as God's continuing activity:

> The world is not something apart from God; it is the medium of His continuing activity...Jesus is not the Christ because of his own goodness or power but because God was present in him...It is the wonder of Jesus that he gave up all claims for himself; he surrendered everything that was Jesus in him to that which was Christ...Jesus steadfastly resisted all temptations to use his union with

---

13. Ibid., 132.
14. Ibid., 178.

God for his own advantage. For Tillich this makes a "Jesus-centered" religion idolatrous.[15]

Actually, a truly Christ-centered religion—in which we see Christ as the central turning point of creation, of history, and of each individual's life—is what we need. This augments our concept of Christ.

The problem is with some of the Jesus-exclusive ideas that arose in the South and elsewhere. These limit our concept of Christ. They also seem to eliminate the Trinity and sometimes even God. Such Jesus-exclusive ideas do verge on idolatry.

Christ is the way to God and cannot be put in the way of God.

Jesus-exclusive ideas have led many people far afield. One example is that of a highly regarded minister and theologian, a veritable patriarch of his denomination. He explained that if we take all parts of the Bible as equally relevant, then we would still be eating kosher foods as the Old Testament commanded, and women would still be wearing hats in church as Paul in the New Testament demanded. Instead, this minister took only what *he* thought was relevant in the Bible and proudly but simplistically concluded, "I pray to Jesus and do as he did."

One little word—*evolution*—and the irrelevance of the Bible falls into place. The Bible is a cumulative narrative of man's spiritual

---

15. Ibid., 186.

Tillich's ideas resonate with mine because of the faith absorbed from my grandmother, Therese Schlennstedt. She was born and schooled in Prussia during the last decades of Melanchthon's school system that included religious instruction. Her life, 1873–1966, outspanned Tillich's. It also spanned a remarkable era that began during the last vestiges of Prussian feudalism, as she referred to *der Gnädige Herr* (the Benevolent Lord) of her childhood. Yet her grandson was an aeronautical engineer who worked on a soil sampler to Mars. She felt for our "poor, innocent moon" but did not live to see the landing on the moon.

evolution through God's continuing revelation of Himself as man was able to understand.

Besides, Jesus never said, "Pray to me." He said to pray in his name. The meaning of a *name*, or a *word*, or *to know* had much more depth in the Bible than for us. The thing known or named or the word spoken were all permeated with, enveloped in, the essence behind it.

The Word of God is the Spirit of God. As Paul noted in Ephesians, "The sword of the Spirit, which is the Word of God" (Eph. 6:17, NIV).

In Revelation, the sword of the Word will prevail—that is, both the Spirit of God and also His words—the little symbols that reflect thoughts and ideas. Jesus himself said that ideas and attitudes cherished in the heart and held in the mind were more important than the law.

8

The Word Unsealed

The Age of Integrity

What are the ideas and attitudes that we hold in our hearts and minds? At present, they are in chaos since we dissected and analyzed everything into bits and pieces. On top of that, we also linger in the last gasps of a sensate culture when "the previous system of value is disintegrated and a new system not yet built, (and) we are faced with social, mental and moral anarchy."[1]

We have seen how twentieth-century "prophets" and intellectuals brought us to this sad state. Now in the twenty-first century, we need to enter the age of integrity when we put our fragmented ideas back together with understanding, wisdom, honesty, integrity—with the integrity of each idea, each individual, each piece, an integral part of the whole of all society

---

1.   Wagar, *The City of Man*, 94.

and all creation—and in the process, see that *everything* is related to God.

During the 1950s, the New American Library published a series called *The Mentor Philosophers*. Each book of the series covered an "age" through the writings of noted philosophers of the time.

Age of Belief. After Augustine put God at the center of the universe and Christianity laid the foundation of Western civ, other religious thinkers laid the steps to reform. Writers, besides Augustine, were Boethius, Abelard, Bernard, Aquinas, Duns Scotus, and William of Ockham.

Age of Adventure. Spanish and Portuguese navigators discovered America and circled the globe. Other thinkers interpreted the heavens. The Renaissance was emphasized as it put humanity at the center of the universe. The Reformation was neglected and also the idea of the "priesthood of the believer," which helped each individual to think for himself. The writers of the age included Da Vinci, More, Machiavelli, Erasmus, Copernicus, Montaigne, Kepler, and Galileo.

Age of Reason. Seventeenth century. Modern science and math made strides. The thinkers included Bacon, Galileo, Pascal, Hobbes, Descartes, Spinoza, and Leibniz.

Age of Enlightenment. Eighteenth century. Reason became supreme, and man, with reason, would create a better world all by himself. But they failed to see (as Bruckberger did) that the United States was founded with input from both the Enlightenment and the Reformation's priesthood of the believer. If you can think for yourself in religious matters, why not also in political? Plus, the idea that "rights" derive from God, not the nation. The writers who made contributions to the age were Locke, Berkeley, Voltaire, Hume, Reid, Condillac, Hamann.

Age of Ideology. Nineteenth century. A world of *isms* arose to clash in the twentieth century. The writers were Kant,

Comte, Mill, Spencer, Marx, Nietzsche, Kierkegaard, Hegel, and Schopenhauer.

Age of Analysis. Twentieth century. Knowledge was dissected and analyzed into bits and pieces. Some men of the age were Bergson, Whitehead, James, Croce, Russell, Dewey, Sartre, and Santayana.

Age of Integrity. Twenty-first century. Now we need to put our world and ideas back together with integrity. The age of integrity is certainly the next logical age. So how do we get integrity? And what is truth? Many people say we cannot really know. It is all relative. Yes, but relative to what? Truth is relative to God—the one absolute that is certain, sure, steadfast, and eternal. But we do not seem to understand this yet.

Warren Wagar in his *City of Man* identified the crisis of the twentieth century as "conceptual chaos…the failure of the knowledge-seeking disciplines to produce a single *unified picture of the world*…like the pieces of a puzzle scattered on a table top."[2]

He saw the scattered pieces of confusion but failed to provide the "picture" on the puzzle-box top. Instead, his solution for our problem (which many people subscribe to) was a "committee with the willingness to agree." Hitler and his cohorts had a willingness to agree. Stalin and his politburo had a willingness to agree. And many others of that ilk.

It is doubtful if a "committee" from Congress, the European Union, the United Nations, our elite universities, or the World Council of Churches is the solution. Although many people would like to be on that committee, it would put too much power in one group. We cannot concentrate power in any committee or group, no matter how high-minded they profess to be.

---

2. Ibid., 95, 174.

Lord Acton said, "Power corrupts, and absolute power corrupts absolutely." That is why our founding fathers wanted a balance of power between three functioning branches of government.

Eric Hoffer (longshoreman-philosopher of 1960s) said, "Dispersion of power is the only check to power there is." This dispersion is what the Reformation and the age of integrity will ultimately provide when each individual—and the church—thinks for itself again.

Dietrich Bonhoeffer *did* think for the church in his book on ethics, which he never finished because he was executed in a Nazi prison just before it was liberated by the United States in 1945. He got to the heart of truth. His ideas on truth were not accepted in the 1940s, but the time now is urgent.

> Telling the truth…is not solely a matter of moral character, it is also a matter of the *correct appreciation of real situations* and of serious reflection upon them. The more complex the actual situation of a man's life, the more responsible and the more difficult will be his task of "telling the truth."
>
> "Telling the truth" must be learned…the *ethical cannot be detached from reality*, and consequently continual progress in learning to *appreciate reality* is a necessary ingredient of *ethical action*.[3]

This seems a bit abstract. Bonhoeffer put it into practice when he truthfully appraised the "reality" of Hitler's Germany, which the German people had allowed to rise. When he came to the United States to teach at a seminary, he could have stayed and been safe. Instead, he said, "The sin of respectable people reveals itself in flight from responsibility." Or in simply closing our eyes to it.

---

3. The source of Bonhoeffer's quotes has been lost.

Bonhoeffer went back to face the reality of the situation in Germany and "his responsibility" in it. He became part of a group who took the "ethical action" of trying to assassinate Hitler. Their first attempt fell apart. On the second attempt, the bomb went off—at a table where Hitler sat with other men. Some died, but not Hitler.

In prison, Bonhoeffer wrote on the "correct appreciation of real situations":

> If one is to say how a thing really is, that is, if one is to speak truthfully, one's gaze and one's thought must be directed toward the way the real exists in God and through God and for God.

In his next quote, Bonhoeffer seemed to echo Romans 1:18–20:

> The lie is primarily the denial of God as He has evidenced Himself to the world...The lie is the denial, the negation and the conscious and deliberate destruction of the reality which is created by God...which consists in God...no matter whether this purpose is achieved by speech or by silence.

Or by telling half the truth. Eric Hoffer observed that "the slickest way to lie is to tell half the truth"—much used by politicians.

Telling the truth in Bonhoeffer's way is important in everything, including or especially in prayer. If we take a problem to God, we have to be honest about it because God already knows the truth of the situation. This is more or less what repenting is. You acknowledge what you contributed to the situation. God really cannot help us unless we admit, confess, acknowledge the truth. This is a big part of prayer—facing up to the truth—because only then can a solution be given to us. God's solution, the only one that works.

This also puts integrity at the core of our being, of our character, and is actually the only way we can truly affirm our *self*. This is the way Bonhoeffer put it. "I can find unity with myself only in surrender of my ego to God—and to men."

The integrity, the authentic true self of a person, comes only when he merges his will with God's will, his spirit with God's Spirit. This means that we have to let God become sovereign in our lives, sovereign in the individual. Of course, we can always say no because God gave us the *free will* to say yes or no to Him. If we say no, God will try to reach us. But finally, He will leave us alone. He will "give us over to ourselves"—to our own stupidity (as in Romans 1:19–34).

In the long run, it is easier and wiser to say yes to God and to the blessings He has planned for us, which naturally follow from living sensibly, according to His Word. Yet the greatest blessing is inner peace, contentment, peace of mind.

The church does not emphasize this peace, this "earthly salvation" of the individual. Yet a world filled with such spiritual individuals remains the unfulfilled promise of the Reformation because the churches have neglected the individual in their emphasis on social action.

Maybe Carl Jung's insights from the 1950s will finally be heard:

> People go on blithely organizing and believing in the sovereign remedy of mass action. Curiously enough, the churches too want to avail themselves of mass action... the very churches whose care is the *salvation of the individual soul*...an individual becomes morally and spiritually inferior in the mass. If the individual is not truly regenerated in spirit, society cannot be either, for society is the sum total of individuals in need of redemption...inner man remains unchanged no matter how much community

he has…Environment cannot give what comes only with effort, *a deep seated change of inner man.*[4]

This change comes when each individual says yes to God and lets God become sovereign in his life. This is what the Reformation was about with its priesthood of the believer—after all, we are made in the image of God.

Julian Hartt (in his book *The Lost Image of Man*) feared we had lost that image. Maybe his insights from the 1960s will finally be heeded.

> Man is a singular creature. He can be undone by the misfiring of his own purposes…because he wrongly (envisions) the good…because he can tell persuasive lies to himself and live with and love even the most violently distorted images of himself as if they were perfect expressions of truth…Man alone has been endowed with the ambiguously valued talent for tricking and lying himself into oblivion.[5]

It is our choice. Integrity—with and through God's truth, as Bonhoeffer explained? Or oblivion?

Beyond Individual Integrity

The integrity of each individual is not sufficient to produce the age of integrity that we need to enter in the twenty-first century.

As stated in the previous section, we need to put our world and our ideas back together with understanding, wisdom, honesty, and integrity—the integrity of each idea, each piece, each individual, integrated into the whole of all society and all creation—and in

---

4. Carl Jung, *Undiscovered Self* (New York: American Library, 1959), 68.
5. Hartt, *The Lost Image of Man,* 124

the process, see that everything is related to God, the one absolute that is certain, sure, steadfast, and eternal.

As Bonhoeffer put it, "I can find unity with myself only in surrender of my ego to God—and to men."

When we have this unity—integrity—when we are at one with God, when we surrender ourselves to God, and let God become sovereign in our lives, *then* we can reach out to others, to our neighbors, as Jesus put it in his two commandments. "Love God with all your heart and strength, mind and soul. And your neighbor as yourself." Each individual who loves God with his entire being and sees God's reality then becomes an integral part of the whole of all society and all creation—the way God intended.

God's way, God's plan, *is* unfolding in the world, as already seen in the two underlying supertrends that seem opposite but are really complementary:[6]

1. The trend toward more *individuality, diversity,* and *plurality* with more freedom
2. The trend toward increasing *interdependence* of individuals, organizations, and nations

E pluribus unum was our motto at one time: "Out of many, one." This is the kind of unity we tried to achieve years ago when we believed that the United States was a melting pot. Now we are a salad. Each ethnic piece is separate and distinct. Tossed together but never blended, for all our multicultural differences must be recognized and emphasized—even enshrined. Yet what we really need to do is rise above our ethnicity, above the tribe, to a prior relation, a prior allegiance to God.

When Abraham was asked to sacrifice Isaac (as explained by Soren Kierkegaard in *Fear and Trembling),* Abraham was asked to rise above the universal ethic of his day, which was the family

---

6. Max Ways, *Fortune* (October 1970).

or tribe. Anything you did to save the tribe was all right. But in the test that God put to Abraham, he was to put his relation to God above everything else, which he did in that instance of the intended sacrifice of Isaac.

Afterward, Abraham became the father of a tribe through Isaac, the Hebrews; and the father of another tribe through Ishmael, the Arabs. Tribes were important then because the world was still in the tribal stage of social development. Tribes served a purpose for most of history—until today. Now one of the biggest problems in the world *is* tribalism—in Africa, in the Israeli-Palestinian conflict, in the whole Middle East situation, and elsewhere.

Someone interviewed one of Osama bin Laden's brothers on television and finally asked him, "If you had the chance, would you turn in Osama?" The brother hedged. He did not want to come right out and say no, but you could see his tribal loyalty was too strong.

Remember the Unabomber? His brother finally put the pieces together and tipped off the FBI. Why? Because there *is* a higher allegiance than tribal loyalty. Our first loyalty is always to God— to stand up for what is right in God's sight, for what is right according to God's truth, God's reality, the big picture.

Feodor Dostoevsky (Russian writer) was talking about the big picture, about humanity and mankind as a whole, when he said, "We arrive—all or none." So we really do need to see the whole picture to see that we are all God's children working together in God's very special creation.

In Genesis, man was in *harmony* with God and creation, until his oneness was broken in the Garden of Eden. His harmony with other people (with society) was also broken in Genesis. The rest of the Bible is about getting back in tune with God, in harmony with God, back to oneness with God—atoned by Christ so we may be at one with God, with ourselves, with society, and with creation.

The word *sympathy*, rather than *harmony*, was used in a doctrine traced back to Hippocrates: "There is one common flow, one common breathing, all things are in sympathy."

Instead of *sympathy* or *harmony*, *unity* was the word used by Pico della Mirandola in the 1800s.

Firstly, there is the unity in things whereby each thing is at one with itself, consists of itself, and coheres with itself. Secondly, there is the unity where one creature is in unity with the others, and all parts of the world constitute one world.[7]

A footnote said, "Pico's third unity was, unavoidably, the unity of the universe and its Creator."

Henri Bergson (born in Paris, 1859–1941) had somewhat the same idea. He had an uplifting philosophy that people liked and Europeans needed at the turn of the century to 1900. He said that the impetus for life was his famous *élan vital*, the life force. This sounds a bit like the "force" of science fiction. When you cannot talk about religion, you talk about the force. This was about where Europeans were in Bergson's heyday. They had given up on religion but still searched for a force, as Bergson explained:[8]

> As the smallest grain of dust is bound up with our entire solar system...so all organized beings, from the humblest to the highest, from the first origins of life to the time in which we are, and in all places as in all times, do but evidence a single impulsion...all the living hold together and all yield to the same tremendous push.

Bergson's *élan vital*, or life force, *is* God's creative force. Wilhelm Dilthey (died ca. 1900) had a similar idea on the *social* level:

---

7. Arthur Koestler, *The Roots of Coincidence* (New York: Random House, 1972), 106.
8. Masur, *Prophets of Yesterday*, 261.

> Underlying all historical creativity is a feeling for life, *Lebensgefuhl,* that all men share...a higher consciousness [which is really the spiritual]...When life and thought meet, the 'feeling of life' crystallizes into a world picture, *Weltbild,* which is the *unifying element in every civilization.*[9]

A civilization needs a "commonly held view of the world to hold it together." At the start of Western civ, that view was Augustine's idea which put God at the center of the universe. Today the world desperately needs a unifying element that will tie all the people of the world together. We need a commonly held worldview (Dilthey's *Weltanschauung*). We are tied together technologically, but we need to have an underlying idea, a philosophy—dare we say a theology?—that will integrate all nations and people and fulfill Revelation's prediction that "all nations, all people, will come to the mountain of the house of the LORD and worship God"—with God at the center of the universe, not man.

Incidentally, the mountain of the house of the Lord is not a literal mountain, which Jews still wail at the side of and Arabs built a mosque on top of—over which both still fight. Just let it go. The Romans destroyed the temple, which had been a place of sacrifice. Sacrifice is not needed anymore because Christ was the supreme sacrifice. No other is needed. Instead of the temple, Jews were to focus on the synagogues, their teaching institutions, in each village and to teach. We are too.[10] As Jesus told the Samaritan

---

9. Ibid., 268–272.
10. Michael Stone, in his article "Judaism at the Time of Christ," *Scientific American* (January 1973), pointed out that of all the Jewish sects at the time of Christ, the only two that survived and flourish today are the Rabbinic Judaism of the synagogues and Christianity, which has since separated from Judaism and has separated into many sects. Will the next round of survivors be the ones who actually teach God's Word, God's truth?

woman at the well, "God is spirit and his worshippers must worship in spirit and truth." God's truth, as Bonhoeffer explained. Dilthey concluded,

> The units which interact (or integrate) in the marvelous complex whole of history and society are individuals— each of which is distinct from every other, each of which is a world.[11]

Each individual *is* distinct. But this is not the selfish, hedonistic individuality of the past five decades. "I can do whatever I please. It's my life. It's my body." When we are young, we feel invincible. But we do pay later for those coffin nails we smoked or whatever else we did that was stupid.

When our daughter was in high school, she worked in the office running errands to earn points for the Honor Society. A sophomore boy overdosed on drugs and became a vegetable overnight. She couldn't believe it. "But I just took a note to him last week." Our body is a temple—not to be trashed, defiled, abused, or misused. For our sake. And for society's sake. Who is going to take care of that boy who foolishly blew his mind with drugs?

The "distinct individuals" Dilthey talked about must be individuals with integrity. Spiritual integrity. Imagine what the world would be like if everyone just picked up after himself. People would not make a mess in the first place. If someone did, he would clean up his own litter and his own problems—with help maybe, but with effort on his part. The Bible says we are to carry one another's burdens. We are to help one another, but everyone carries. No one is absolved.

In Alaska, on a paddle wheeler out of Fairbanks, a native guide explained the big fish wheels in the river. Then she added her own remembrance. When the fish traps were full, her whole family

---

11. Ibid.

went down to the river and carried the fish up the hill for the fish to be dried. When she was two or three years old, she was given a small fish that may or may not have made it up the hill. At two, she could not do anything worthwhile, but she got the idea of contributing to her family, her society. By the time she was five, she and her brother managed to carry a "sizeable tub of fish between them."

Each individual contributes to society—to the best of one's ability. In the Middle Ages, when the first cathedrals were built, they were finely crafted even in the uppermost finials that no eye could see. The best that a craftsman could give in service to God. People saw their work as a tribute to God, and they put their best into it, no matter whether anyone else saw it or not. Just imagine if we thought and worked like that today!

Yet we need this kind of integrity throughout society, for society works both ways—from the bottom up and top down—and needs integrity throughout. People will get the kind of government they deserve and demand. Individuals do have to assume responsibility, with integrity and morality, to live decent lives and to hold their leaders to high standards. If individuals abdicate responsibility, they will have dictators who control people according to their own whim.

Many people in Eastern Europe did *not* want to give up communism, which had taken over responsibility for the individual. After the Berlin Wall fell in 1989, the mayor of Leipzig (actually the president of the city council) came to Houston, its new "sister city." He was a Lutheran minister and was instrumental in the wall's fall—from the other side. He started prayer meetings, which was the only way more than twenty-five people could gather. More and more people met in more and more cities. Thousands of people met to pray, even nonreligious ones. After a while, the people wanted to move against the wall, but the minister cautioned them to wait for fear of bloodshed.

When the time was right, the people simply *overwhelmed* the wall. Without bloodshed!

In his speech in Houston, the Leipzig minister said some East Germans did not want the wall down and did not want reunification. In September 2004, a survey found that 20 percent of East Germans still did not want the wall down. They do not want the responsibility. For as Julian Hartt explained, "Freedom is a dreadful burden, if it means that a man is absolutely responsible for himself and can really and finally be only what he is prepared to resolve to become."[12]

In his January 2005 inaugural address, President George W. Bush said, "Self-government, in the end, relies on the governing of the self." A paternalistic society or nanny state may seem enticing, but does it work for the good of the people? In the long run?

On the other hand, when the reins of communism were loosened, many people took advantage of the situation. Corruption ran rampant in Russia. In Mexico and South America, many people suffer from government corruption. In Africa, most problems, starvation and suffering, are caused by the corruption of leaders in government. The United Nations is also tainted with corruption.

Transparency International is a group that was organized several years ago with headquarters in Berlin. The idea behind the group is that transparency in government will make it more open and more honest and get rid of corruption. Over one hundred nations belong. *The Wall Street Journal* had a chart that ranked the nations. Scandinavian countries were at the top. Many others need help. And even more need to belong.

But even if we get transparency, honesty, and integrity spread throughout society, we still have not finished the job before us in the age of integrity.

---

12. Hartt, *The Lost Image of Man*, 100

An Integral Part of Creation

A number of years ago, Jaroslav Pelikan stated, "The two biggest problems facing Christianity today are the dichotomy of the individual in society and of society in creation."[13]

In the past, we made the individual in society an either-or situation, thus the dichotomy. Yet even if individuals of integrity become integral parts of society, we still need to fit each individual and all of society into the whole of creation. That is the dichotomy there.

Each person has an impact on God's creation. In Genesis, man was given dominion to be stewards of God's creation. Dominion and stewardship mean to cultivate, to take care of, not to exploit.

A real-estate developer once said, "I'll take any piece of land I can get hold of and cut it up and sell it." That is a bit too enterprising. We do *not* need to cover every square foot with concrete. We are to use God's creation wisely and leave the earth better than we found it. Of course, some environmentalists do go to the opposite extreme.

Even beyond our care and tending of the earth, people need an underlying feeling of closeness to God's creation. This closeness was easier when people lived on the land in the agricultural stage. It is an awareness that many city people lose, but our survival may depend on keeping it and renewing it.

Decades ago, Frank Lloyd Wright, the architect, said, "If grass isn't growing on Fifth Avenue in ten years, we are doomed." Maybe New York is, but not those of us still out in the hinterlands—not yet anyway.

Ever since the Tower of Babel in Genesis, man has come under God's unwritten law of civilization. The builders at Babel

---

13. Jaroslav Pelikan is a Lutheran theologian. In 2003, his book *Credo* was published. It is a guide to Christian creeds and confessions of faith. His new book in 2005 is *Whose Bible Is It?*

became overawed with the tower *they* built, so they were doomed to leave amid a jumble of languages. It was with Babel's dawn and doom that the rise and fall of civilization came into being. British historian Arnold Toynbee used a rise-fall theme when he wrote his *History of Civilization.* He identified about twenty-one.

But the first rise-fall theory was put forth by Islamic historian Ibn Khaldun (1332–1406) when he saw the impending fall of his own civilization, ca. 1400. This was about the same time Europeans were taking their first steps to the Reformation. Unfortunately, Islam did not have the reform they needed just as badly as Christianity did. Both Western and Islamic civs were one thousand years into civilization. The Reformation saved Western civilization through its dynamic shift to America and to the United States.

According to Khaldun's rise-fall theory, nomads accustomed to hard living produced a rise while the corruption of luxury and softness destined a fall.

Now we can see that a dynamic rise comes when society moves from the country to the city, from the agrarian stage into manufacturing and trade, which matures into an industrial-commercial economy then finally moves into a financial stage with wealth and luxury like ours. Wealth produces the flowering of civilization with money to fund education, arts, etc. But in the process, when society gets too far from the land, too far from God's creation, when society becomes too enamored with luxury and with what *man* has created—enamored with his own tower of Babel—he *is* doomed to fall.

Are we headed for a fall? Or will we remain close to God's creation and fit into it with respect and awe? For it is truly awesome, especially when we see those pictures from space of our beautiful blue-and-white Earth.

This earth, this world, is ours. In trust. Will we acknowledge that God has entrusted *His* creation to us?

A Symbolic Revelation

Since this book is a study of the Bible in the context of history, we must revisit the Revelation to John, for it is now reaching fulfillment. This is not a surrealistic "wait on a mountaintop, for the end is near" type of conclusion. We must move beyond the surreal interpretations of the past. God has always met us in simple, everyday events, and He will now. If we understand the importance of ideas and concepts, including the depth of meaning behind names and words, then the cryptic words of Revelation will be *unsealed*.

As stated earlier, the Revelation assured persecuted Christians of the absolute sovereignty of God and ultimate destruction of evil (including Satan) after much tribulation. In the meantime, there is spiritual inner peace for those who are faithful to God and the Lamb. In the end, there is the promise of fulfillment with the Second Coming of the Lord Jesus and a new Jerusalem where all people will know God. This is the overall message. Now for a few specifics.

Scholars once thought that John the apostle wrote Revelation. Tradition said John taught at a "seminary" in Ephesus, which served churches in Asia Minor. He suffered persecution when emperor worship was revived. One persecution was at the time of Nero in the 60s, when Peter was executed in Rome. During this time, Vespasian was a general sent to Judea to bring order, but he was called back to Rome to become emperor, 69 to79. Son Titus finished the mop-up in Judea, including destruction of the temple in Jerusalem. Titus ruled for two years, followed by second son, Domitian, 81 to 96, who enforced a new persecution (the three were the Flavian dynasty).

Domitian's persecution sent John to Patmos. John the apostle would have been too old by then, so another John was probably the one who was exiled. We do not know what John's situation was on Patmos, although tour guides probably have caves and rock foundations of houses to show people. Wherever or whoever he was, John evidently had plenty of papyrus and ink stashed away for the scrolls he wrote (books were invented in the next century).

One Sunday morning, John was "in the spirit" at his worship. A voice like a trumpet interrupted him. John turned to the voice. He saw seven lamp stands. Among them was a being that looked like a man. This person was a completely *symbolic figure*. In fact, Revelation is more symbolic than real. It is apocalyptic. And cryptic. It was encoded so only Christians could understand the message. In fact, it was so bizarre and far-out that other people, especially Romans, would think it was ridiculous and ignore it.[14]

A few encryption hints help us understand the symbolism.

- Angels are messengers of God the Holy Spirit.
- Lamp stands are churches.
- The number seven is used fifty-two times. Seven is a complete number, the sum of three and four.
- The number three is heaven, the Trinity.
- The number four relates to four corners of the earth (i.e., the four directions: north, south, east, west).
- Three times four equals twelve, an important number. Twelve tribes. Twelve apostles. Square that, $12 \times 12 = 144$, a more important number. Then add zeros for even more power, for example, 144,000.
- Of the 404 verses in Revelation, 278 refer to the Old Testament.

---

14. Recent books about the "rapture" take the symbols literally. The word *rapture* is not in the Bible. A woman in England, ca. 1835, came up with the word. A century and half later, a newsclip about the "rapture books" reported that the British were surprised at Americans for believing in the rapture.

- Also, there are seven blessings in Revelation: 1:3, 14:13, 16:15, 19:9, 20:6, 22:7, 22:14.

Back to the figure John saw. He was "like the Son of Man" and in *symbolic* dress.

- White robe is Jesus as high priest.
- Gold sash is authority.
- White hair is wisdom, dignity.
- "Eyes like blazing fire" relates to eyes with penetrating insight.
- "Feet of burnished bronze" is strength, stability, steadfastness (no feet of clay).
- "Voice like rushing water" is a phrase Ezekial used to describe God.
- "In his right hand, he held seven stars" which are seven angels of seven churches. The right hand is the symbol of God's providence and means Christ will lead seven churches that represent all churches.
- "Out of his mouth a double-edged sword" is divine judgment. *Sword of mouth* and *sword of word* mean that words and ideas will prevail over swords of war.
- "Face like a sun shining in brilliance" is the full glory of God, from whom illumination and revelation come.

John was *impressed*. He fell as though dead. The figure like Jesus touched him. "Do not be afraid. Write what you have seen, what is now and what will be later" (Rev. 1:17,19, NIV).

John sat down and started to write. He probably used Paul as a model then outdid Paul because John started with a prologue, greetings, doxology, and a small poem. After all this preliminary, John related his experiences of the morning.

Then he recorded a special message to each of the seven churches. The seven are a cross section of the church universal so the messages apply to all churches. Each letter starts with "This message is from one who." It takes one of the attributes from the figure among the lamp stands and uses it to identify Himself. Each letter ends with "He who has ears, let him hear and heed." There is also a promise of eternal life that comes either before or after the hear-heed admonition.

1. *Ephesus* was a port city that is now too far inland to be a port, so it has good ruins with a temple to Diana. Their message: You have worked hard. You do not tolerate evil. You test for false teaching. You hate Nicolaitans (quasi-Christians who added pagan ideas—some were Gnostic, with the belief that it did not matter what you did with the body if the soul was all right). You suffered for my sake. That is all well and good. *But* you have slacked off and grown weary. You need reconvicting with your original passion.

2. *Smyrna* was forty miles north of Ephesus. It is the present port city of Ismer, or Izmer, the third largest city in Turkey after Istanbul and Ankara. Ismer was built on top of old Smyrna, so there are few ruins. Those few ruins include a temple to the emperor. Their message had no condemnation, just encouragement, as they went through trials and the tribulation of friction between Jews and Christians, plus persecution.

3. *Pergamum* was the city where Galen, the Greek physician, lived, so medicine was important with a temple to Aesculapius, the symbol of doctors. A century later, men in Pergamum introduced parchment and bound books as we know them. Their message recognized that they were faithful, even though they lived where Satan had his throne with an altar to Zeus. They were cautioned to beware of immorality and people with pagan ideas and idols, also Nicolaitans.

4. *Thyatira* was a manufacturing center for copper, textiles, and dyes. Lydia, the "dyer of purple" who helped Paul, was from here. Thyatira had a temple to Apollo. Their message expressed appreciation for their love, faithfulness, service, patience, and growth in all of these. But they had a Jezebel who needed to be rooted out, so they were to hold fast and root her out.

5. *Sardis* was the capital of ancient Lydia with king Midas of the golden touch and rich king Croesus. Lydians invented coins for trade. They had a temple to Artemis. The message for the church was one of accusation: You are a bunch of hypocrites. You act like you are alive, but you are dead. Wake up and strengthen what you have before it dies completely.

6. *Philadelphia* was located at a gateway in the mountains to the high central plains of "Asia," actually to eastern Turkey, then to Asia. They received no reprimand: You are small with little power, but you have an open door of opportunity to the east. Spread the message as you hold fast to what you have.

7. *Laodicea* was the wealthiest city in the area with banks, textiles, a medical school, and "eye salve." There were no good words for them, only condemnation. Laodicea was neither hot nor cold, even though they had hot springs and cold from mountain snows. They felt they were rich and had all they needed, but they were poor, naked (vulnerable), and blind in spite of the eye salve. Repent and sit with Me and My Father. He, who has ears, let him hear and heed.

The seven churches evidently heard and heeded. The area became a center of Christianity and provided the underlying unity and dynamic thrust to the Christian empire that emerged two centuries later, when Constantine made Christianity the state religion of the Roman Empire.

The Spiritual Revealed

So far, Revelation was rather ordinary, everyday preaching, the here and now of *what is*. Chapters 4 and 5 of Revelation introduce *what is to come*. John saw a "door open to heaven." This meant that John saw the spiritual revealed.

The voice like a trumpet, which was the first voice John had heard, said, "Come up here and I will show what must take place after this." (Some interpreters find the rapture here. Let's stick with "come see the spiritual revealed" as in a vision.) At once, John was in the spirit and had a vision that provided him with *spiritual insight*.

John saw a bright figure on a bright throne, which *symbolized* God and His sovereignty. God was attended by an inner circle of four creatures like a lion, an ox, a man, and an eagle. These represented God's creation and came before the time of the twenty-four elders in the outer circle. The elders (twelve tribes and twelve apostles) were dressed in white and wore gold crowns and sat on thrones—when they were not on their knees bowing down.

God held a scroll in His *right* hand. The scroll was "written within and on the back" and had seven seals that no one could open. John wept, but one of the elders comforted him. "Do not weep. Jesus can open the scroll and seven seals." The Word will be unsealed.

A Lamb, who was at the throne, took the scroll amid much singing and many amens. If, while studying Revelation, you hear a performance of Handel's "Messiah" with organ, chorus, and orchestra, you know how John must have felt looking through the door open to heaven.

The Lamb, Jesus, opened the seals to reveal the tribulations that were to come between John's first century and our twentieth.

Chapters 6 to 16 tell what will happen during this interim. The tribulations come in three sets of seven seals, seven trumpets, and seven bowls. These are awful, but interludes of reprieve and reassurance are interspersed in and between the three sets, between the seals and trumpets, then between the trumpets and bowls.

Chapter 12 is an interlude between the trumpets and bowls. Entitled "The Woman and the Dragon," the message is quite confusing until we see that the woman is the Judeo-Christian faith through the ages. The dragon is everything against her, whatever its name.

The woman had a crown with twelve stars, which represent the twelve tribes of Judaism, from whom Jesus came. The woman gave birth to a son. When the dragon tried to devour him—crucify him—he was taken to God and His throne, where Christ now sits at God's right hand (as we repeat every time we say the Apostle's Creed).

The woman, who now represents Christianity, fled to a desert (a desert is a place of refuge in the Bible). Through the Roman conquest of Western Europe, God prepared a place of refuge for Christianity, for this is where Christianity laid the foundation of Western civilization a few centuries later. The church was led to this new place of refuge in Europe, when Peter went to Rome and when Paul was sent to Macedonia instead of Asia (Acts 16:9).

Again, the dragon pursued the woman. She was given the wings of a huge eagle and flew to a new refuge where she was renewed and safe from the dragon for three and a half times. Christianity with the wings of an eagle flew from Europe to America, represented by the eagle. There it was safe and renewed for three and a half times. The time units are centuries. Thus, during the seventeenth, eighteenth, nineteenth, and half of the twentieth century, Christianity was safe and thrived in America, for America was discovered just in time to provide a *refuge* for Protestants. There they founded a new nation based on the reformed Judeo-Christian tradition.

Then the dragon was enraged at the woman and went off to make war against the rest of her offspring—those who obey God's commandments and hold to the testimony of Jesus. (Rev. 12:17, NIV)

In the last half of twentieth century since the 1960s, Christianity and Western civilization have been put down, ridiculed, denigrated, even reviled and vilified.

Then from his mouth the dragon spewed water like a river to overtake the woman and sweep her away with the torrent. But the earth helped the woman by opening its mouth and swallowing the river that the dragon had spewed. (Rev. 12:15–16, NIV)

The "dragon spewed deceit, misinformation and derision" in a torrent to sweep away the woman, but all this was swallowed up by the earth, for in the new world, people on each new frontier were forced into a down-to-earth existence with a renewed closeness to the earth and to God's creation. This kept them close to God and to their Judeo-Christian faith.

From personal experience, I know this is true. When I was eleven, we lived in Austin. My father was offered an appointment in Washington, DC, but my mother refused to go. She was an only child and did not want to be that far from her parents. So we moved to the family farm near a very small town. When I was a senior in high school (a bleak time in the middle of World War II when *everything* was rationed and *every* boy was in the service), I was walking down our lane to the road for the school bus. At the middle gate, I told the air, the wind, whatever would listen, "I have not had one advantage by moving to the country—not *one* single advantage." From out of nowhere, the words came to me— *except a closeness to God.* Immediately, I realized I would not have had this closeness in Washington. I may or may not have had it in Austin, but I certainly had it in the country. And compared to that, what else matters?

I now know it was closeness to God's creation and to God the Creator that I absorbed while living on the farm. The United States has always had a last frontier where people remained close to God's creation. Texas is now that last frontier where many people, even those in cities, have kept their ties to the land.

The torrent spewed by the dragon certainly describes the situation in the world today. The world is so full of deceit and misinformation, distortions of truth, even malicious slander. Is it any wonder that our ideas are in chaos and we have so much dissension? It is hard for anyone to remain grounded in the truth, in the reality of Bonhoeffer's truth.

The Sword of the Word

In chapter 13, the dragon that pursued the woman then stood on the shore of a sea. John saw a beast coming out of the sea. This beast represents knowledge, as the beast and serpent do in Genesis. In the Bible, the "sea" or the "deep" represent chaos. So the beast in the sea is knowledge in chaos. The conceptual chaos of the twentieth century. We need to bring order out of conceptual chaos and see that ultimately, all knowledge is *of* God to know God.

The dragon gave power to the beast of the sea, and people worshipped the dragon and the beast except those who belong to the Lamb (paraphrased from Revelation13:2 and 8, NIV).

The dragon (those against the church) allied with knowledge, and people worshipped the dragon and the beast, except for faithful Christians. We need to understand that knowledge is from God to know God and is *good*. But we are not to worship knowledge or intellectualism or twist it to fit our designs.

Finally, the bowls of wrath were poured out. As the angel poured out the seventh bowl, a voice from the throne said, "It is done." After the seventh bowl comes the end of the evil world system represented by the harlot Babylon. The evils of civilization will be drowned like a millstone thrown into the sea. The prostituted glories ascribed to civilization and to society will fall away when seen in the true light of God and the lamp of Christ illuminating truth.

Chapter 17 of Revelation was discussed earlier, at the time it was written. When persecuted Christians in Rome needed assurance that Rome would fall, they were given the picture of a woman riding a beast in a sea of chaos (Rev. 17:4–10).

The woman had *Babylon* stamped on her forehead. Babylon represented the worst evils of civilization to the Jews, so she is civilization. The beast is knowledge. In Genesis, the words *Eve*, *serpent*, *reveal*, and *beast* are similar. The serpent represented wisdom or knowledge. Now applied to Roman civilization, the woman is seated on the beast with seven heads, which are the seven hills of Rome. They are also seven kings or seven civilizations that accumulated mankind's fund of knowledge. The five already fallen were those that the Hebrews came in contact with in BC centuries: 1) Sumerian, 2) Egyptian, 3) Babylonian, 4) Persian, 5) Hellenic. The one that *is* and was implied to fall was 6) Roman. The one "yet to come" (in a direct line of ascent) and to stay "only a little while" is 7) Western civilization.

In the meantime, the angel explained to John, "The waters you saw where the harlot is sitting, are people and multitudes and nations and languages" (Rev. 17:15, RSV).

The people and nations of the world are in chaos. Social chaos. "Languages in the waters" means that our ideas are in chaos too. Conceptual chaos.

So it is time for the harlotry of Babylon to cease, time for the evils of civilization to be "drowned like a millstone thrown into the sea" (Rev. 18:21, RSV). And it is time for the kingdom of God to come to fulfillment on earth. The prostituted glories that we ascribe to civilization and to society will fall away when seen in the true light of God and the lamp of Christ illuminating truth—in the reality that Bonhoeffer urged.

John again heard multitudes of hallelujahs. He was so overwhelmed he forgot to write. He even started to bow down to the angel emissary, who cautioned him,

> Do not do it! I am a fellow servant with you and with your brothers who hold to the testimony of Jesus. Worship God! For the testimony of Jesus is the spirit of prophecy. (Rev. 19:10, niv)

The spirit of prophecy is the spirit of the future, of Christ at the right hand of God leading God's providence in history. John saw "heaven standing open." The spiritual was completely revealed. John saw a white horse:

> The rider on the white horse was called Faithful and True. He has a name written on him. His name is the *Word of God*. Out of his mouth comes a sharp sword with which to strike down nations. (Excerpts from Revelation 19:12–15, niv)

The wrongs of the nations will be righted by the man on the white horse. Another name is written on his robe and his thigh: "King of kings and Lord of lords." This means the wrongs will be righted by the truth that comes from the mouth of the rider, whose name is the Word of God. The Word become flesh will bring order out of social chaos.

"Birds" are invited to come watch as nations and the beast and the false prophet are defeated by the sword of him on the white horse, by the sword that issues from his mouth. The sword of the Word of God will conquer the world. One must pause to grasp the full import and portent of this statement. The *Word* of God will conquer. Way back in Isaiah, God said,

> So shall my Word be that goes forth from my mouth; it
> shall not return to me empty, but it shall accomplish that
> which I purpose. (Isa. 55:11, RSV)

The Word is God's will, God's spirit, God's providence, and God's scripture.

Almost abruptly, to conclude and end this time of tribulation, Satan is dispensed with in Revelation 20. He will be bound for a thousand years then loosed for a while and finally tossed in the fiery lake with the beast and false prophet. Remember, Satan did not come into the Bible until Job, probably after contact with the Persians, ca. 500 BC. This was after Zoroaster's dualism, which continued in Manichaean ideas, which Augustine subscribed to until he was converted to Christianity ca. AD 400. So Augustine knew whereof he spoke when he refuted dualism by saying that evil is not a force in itself, but *a lack of conformity* to God's will. His ideas held Satan in check for a while (for a thousand years). By the time of Dante's *Divine Comedy* with its *Inferno*, Satan was certainly loose again ca. 1400.

The idea of Satan and his brimstone pit probably served a purpose by scaring a bit of morality into people. But now no purpose is served, just the opposite. Satanic cults serve no one, nor does the excuse of blaming an outside force when evil resides in the minds of men. In Genesis, after the flood, God said, "Never again will I curse the ground because of man, even though every inclination of his heart is evil from childhood" (Gen. 8:21, NIV). And from childhood, each child needs to be nurtured and trained in the faith. In God's truth.

So it is time to dispense with Satan and consign him to the brimstone pit. Also, purgatory has served its purpose. Now we need to understand that hell begins here on earth. A quote from Johann Wolfgang von Goethe applies here: "*Alle Schult auf Erdens rechts sich.*" (All guilt on earth rights itself.) In time, God's time, there is always "a wry a-righting of the awry."

Surely now, we can understand that "hell" is to be abandoned by God and given over to ourselves.

> Furthermore, since they did not think it worthwhile to retain the knowledge of God, *He gave them over* to a depraved mind, to do what ought not to be done. They have become filled with every kind of wickedness, evil, greed and depravity. They are full of envy, murder, strife, deceit and malice. They are gossips, slanderers, God-haters, insolent, arrogant and boastful; they invent ways of doing evil; they disobey their parents; they are senseless, faithless, ruthless. Although they know God's righteous decree that those who do such things deserve death, they not only continue to do these very things but also approve of those who practice them. (Rom. 1:28–32, NIV)

It *is* time for God's righteousness to return to this earth. The time of tribulation, from John's first century to our twentieth, is now reaching conclusion. After the turn of the millennium, the world should be ready at least to start to move into a new era, into the age of fulfillment.

Close of the Age and Dawn of the New

John had a vision of the new era.

> Then I saw a new heaven and a new earth, for the first heaven and the first earth had passed away, and the sea was no more. (Rev. 21:1, RSV)

The worldly world of the first heaven and the first earth passed away, and the sea of chaos was no more. The sea was smooth as glass. The worldly world was replaced by the Holy City—a *symbolic* New Jerusalem—a spiritually-thinking world that is not a harlot of pseudocivilization but is a bride of Christ, as the spiritual kingdom of God finally comes into being on earth.

God will dwell with men, for the old order of things has passed away. God is making everything new. The angel showed John the Holy City that was represented by a *figurative* New Jerusalem. (There is *no* real estate involved in this city, just symbolism.) The jewel-encrusted city had twelve gates with the names of the twelve tribes of Israel. The wall of the city had twelve foundations with the names of the twelve apostles. The new city, new civilization, will have a Judeo-Christian base.

But there is no temple in the city.

> For its temple is the Lord God the Almighty and the Lamb...for the glory of God is its light, and its lamp is the Lamb. (Rev. 21:22–23, RSV)

There is no temple because the temple had been a place for the sacrifice of all those lambs. Now, after the sacrifice of the Lamb of God, no more animal sacrifices or a temple for their sacrifice will be needed. Also, in the past, the temple had been an object of worship in itself. Now, the revelation and illuminations of God and Christ are the light and lamp that all nations will see by. Instead of temples, there will be teaching centers, such as synagogues and churches. These will reveal the glory of God and the Lamb. These will teach that the basis of all thought and knowledge rests on *acknowledging the Trinity*—God Almighty: Creator, Christ, and Holy Spirit—so that all of society will know and worship God. And all nations will walk in that light, that truth.

The river of the water of life flowed from the throne of God and the Lamb down the middle of the great street of the city. On each side of the river stood the tree of life, yielding fruit for every month and leaves for the healing of nations (Rev. 22:1). The tree of life bearing twelve crops of fruit means that food should be sufficient because different areas of the world will produce crops at different times, as summer fruit from Chile helps the United States in winter. The leaves will provide healing for nations, for there is a soothing balm that pervades a person and will permeate society when mankind again becomes one with God's creation.

Before we continue, I need to weave in my Revelation experience. On a February morning in 1972, I was waiting for my friend Nell to come by and take me to a meeting or a lecture or a luncheon or something. I felt a nudge and heard the words, *Read Revelation.* "I really can't now," I argued. The nudge became a prod, and the words a bit louder, *Read Revelation.* "I know. I know. I plan to read it next week." The prodding waned to a nudge. The words grew fainter, *Read Revelation.*

I could ignore the nudge, and it would go away. It was already fading. But then I might miss what I was to understand. "I do have an hour and *if* I am supposed to read Revelation *now*, then now is the time to do it. And if I plan to read it next week anyway, I may as well do it now" (the willing attitude with which we humans respond).

I sat down at the kitchen table and opened my Good News New Testament. My mind opened too as I questioned, "What can this mean in simple common-sense terms?" I waited for my special message. As I read through chapters, I gathered insight but still no message. When I turned to the last two pages, I thought, rather irreverently, *Almost through and no message yet. God better hurry if He has something for me.* Distracted only for the moment of turning the page, I immediately returned to reading. With intense concentration, I began the section titled "The Coming of Jesus." This coming, the "Second Coming," had always bothered me, so I looked intently at the passage as I read down to the last two lines.

> He who testifies to these things says, "Yes, I am coming soon." Amen. Come Lord Jesus. The grace of the Lord Jesus be with God's people. Amen. (Rev. 22:20–21, NIV)

Lord Jesus. The picture painted by earlier generations was that of a figure in a flowing robe striding across a field of wildflowers. Consider the lilies. People in the past always insisted on a physical return. What about spiritual? He shall return as he left. Are we trying to make a physical thing out of a spiritual? The trouble is with our concepts. Our concepts of the Lord Jesus. Lord means divine. Jesus means human. The idea of a divine human being.

The concept of the Lord Jesus dawned rather tentatively. Then a wave of understanding and assurance swept over me. That's it. That's what I was supposed to see. Here in the next to last verse. He will come again when a full understanding of the Lord Jesus concept comes into all the world. This is the key to whole understanding. For a name, a word, a concept in biblical usage had much more meaning than in our terms. That is why Jesus said, "Pray in my *name*," in the name of Christ, the Lord Jesus.

Thus ends the book of Revelation. "Come, Lord Jesus." *The* Christ, the divine human being, the Son of Man at the right hand of God. All that is embodied in this *name*, in this concept, will permeate our thinking with the Second Coming of the Lord Jesus.

In fact, that *is* the Second Coming—renewed and complete understanding of the First Coming within the whole Trinity.

Finally, we can abandon our surrealistic ideas about the Second Coming. No one has to go out on a hill and wait for a cataclysmic end to the world. God has always revealed Himself in simple, ordinary, everyday experience. What could have been more simple, more everyday, or more beautiful than the First Coming as a babe in a manger? The Second Coming will be just as simple and everyday and inspiring.

We simply need to understand the Lord Jesus concept and all that the name implies, Son of Man at the right hand of God. Plus all that the Trinity implies. This is *the Word unsealed*.

Americans may give this understanding to the world for a new-world spirit as a new era dawns with the twenty-first century because the 2000 BC–AD 2000 period of the Judeo-Christian era is complete. This does not mean that the Judeo-Christian era will be done away with, for the future cannot exist except on that base, on the twelve gates and twelve foundations, on the twelve tribes and twelve apostles. It simply means that we will be shifting into the next level of spiritual development—into a full and *true* understanding of the Trinity that includes *all* the spiritual evolution that has gone before.

Apocalypse to the Hebrews was both an end and a beginning. We are at the end of an age yet at the dawn of a new age of fulfillment through understanding a whole balanced Trinity. In this new world, New Jerusalem, kingdom of God on earth, *all* mankind may worship God and come to the *mountain* of the house of the Lord, as many of the Old Testament prophets foresaw.

More recently than the prophets, a Japanese convert said, "Religion is like climbing Mt. Fujiyama. They all get you part way up, but only Christianity gets you to the top."

Paul foresaw the end of the age in 1 Corinthians 15 (NIV):

> Then the end [of the age] will come, when he hands over the kingdom to God the Father after He has destroyed all dominion, authority and power...For he [Christ] must reign until he has put all his enemies under his feet. (15:24)

Christ has reigned at the right hand of God as Christianity became established and was taken to the ends of the earth. Christianity has been a dominant influence in the world since it became the state religion of the Roman Empire and the foundation of Western civilization. Christ is still at the forefront leading of God's providence.

> The last enemy to be destroyed is death. [That is, the fear of death. If we truly believe in the resurrection, we have nothing to fear.] For he "has put every thing under his feet." Now when it says that "everything" has been put under him, it is clear that this does not include God himself, who put everything under Christ. When he has done this, then the Son himself will be made subject to him who put everything under him, so that *God may be all in all.* (1 Cor. 15:26–28, NIV)

God will be "all in all" when we truly and intimately know God Almighty—Creator, Christ, and Holy Spirit. That is, when we truly comprehend and fully embrace the whole Trinity. Jesus foresaw this in his last words to his disciples.

> All authority in heaven and on earth has been given to me. Therefore go and make disciples of all nations, baptizing them in the name of the Father and of the Son and of the Holy Spirit, and teaching them to obey everything I have commanded you; and surely, I am with always, to the very close of the age. (Matt. 28:18–20, NIV)

We are at the close of the age yet at the dawn of a new age with a new-world spirit, a New Jerusalem, the kingdom of God on earth. Now all mankind may worship God and come to the mountain of the house of the Lord.

We are in a time of fulfillment when we may finally and fully understand the all-encompassing wholeness of one God Almighty who manifested Himself as Creator, Christ, and Holy Spirit. And we may fully understand baptizing in the *name* of the Father, Son, and Holy Spirit.

The whole world may now move into the spiritual realm with a new-world spirit by acknowledging one God and understanding the wholeness of a balanced Trinity for real harmony between man and God (each individual and God), between man and man (each individual and society), and between man and creation. Perhaps we can also see the following:

- The Word of God spoken at creation brought order out of physical chaos.
- The Word became flesh in the Lord Jesus to bring order out of social chaos.
- The Word unsealed will bring order out of conceptual chaos.

Now all people everywhere may understand God's Word and truly know God.

In the beginning was the Word. But the Word needed understanding to accomplish what God purposed—for each of us to know God intimately and personally through the Lord Jesus Christ and all that he was, is, and did for us. So we may *all* be one with God.

For His is the kingdom and the power and the glory forever and ever. Amen.

Bibliography

Albright, William Foxwell, *History, Archeology and Christian Humanism*, McGraw-Hill, 1964

Bainton, Roland, *Here I Stand*, New American Library for Abingdon Press, Nashville, 1978

Barclay, William, *The Gospel of Mark*, The Westminster Press, Philadelphia, 1975

Barfield, Owen, *Saving the Appearances–A Study in Idolatry*, Wesleyan Press, 1988

Barrett, William, *Irrational Man*, Doubleday, 1958

Bonhoeffer, Dietrich

Brinton, Crane, John B. Christopher, Robert Lee Wolff, *A History of Civilization Vol.1 and Vol.2*, Prentice-Hall, Inc., Englewood Cliffs, NJ, 1967

Brown, Harrison, *Challenge of Man's Future*, Viking Press, 1967

Bruckberger, R.L., *Image of America*, The Viking Press, New York, 1959

Easton, Stewart C., *The Heritage of the Past: Earliest Times to 1500*, Holt, Rinehart and Winston, New York, 1970

Fairservis, Walter A. Jr. *The Origins of Oriental Civilization*, Mentor Books, New York, 1959

Freud, Sigmund, *Civilization and Its Discontents,* Norton & Co, 1961

Hamblin, Dora Jane, Has the Garden of Eden Been Located at Last? *Smithsonian,* May, 1987

Hartt, Julian, *The Lost Image of Man,* Louisiana State University Press, 1963

Heer, Friedrich, *Charlemagne and His World,* MacMillan, New York, 1975

Hordern, William, *A Layman's Guide to Protestant Theology,* MacMillan, New York, 1968

Johnson, Paul, *Intellectuals,* Harper & Row, New York, 1988

Jung, Carl, *The Undiscovered Self,* Mentor Books, 1958

Kierkegaard, Soren, *Fear and Trembling,* Princeton University Press, 1969

Koestler, Arthur, *Roots of Coincidence,* Random House, New York, 1972

Lipscomb, Thomas book review of *The Island at the Center of the World,* by Russell Shorto in Wall Street Journal, March 16, 2004

Marshack, Alexander, Exploring the Mind of Ice-Age Man, *National Geographic,* January,1975

Masur, Gerhard, *Prophets of Yesterday–Studies in European Culture, 1890-1914,* MacMillan Co., New York, 1961

Mattingly, Garrett, *The Armada,* Houghton Mifflin Co. Boston, 1959

Newsweek, March 12, 1979, *Probing the Universe.*

Reader's Digest, *Last Two Million Years,* Reader's Digest Association, 1974

Tawney, Richard, *Religion and the Rise of Capitalism,* Mentor, 1950

Tuchman, Barbara, *A Distant Mirror,* Alfred A Knoph, New York, 1978

Wagar, W. Warren, *The City of Man,* Houghton Mifflin Co. Boston, 1963

Ways, Max, *Fortune* Magazine, October, 1970

listen|imagine|view|experience

AUDIO BOOK DOWNLOAD INCLUDED WITH THIS BOOK!

In your hands you hold a complete digital entertainment package. In addition to the paper version, you receive a free download of the audio version of this book. Simply use the code listed below when visiting our website. Once downloaded to your computer, you can listen to the book through your computer's speakers, burn it to an audio CD or save the file to your portable music device (such as Apple's popular iPod) and listen on the go!

How to get your free audio book digital download:

1. Visit www.tatepublishing.com and click on the e|LIVE logo on the home page.
2. Enter the following coupon code:
   045a-1fb3-d059-ec8d-beef-a2a4-b616-e511
3. Download the audio book from your e|LIVE digital locker and begin enjoying your new digital entertainment package today!